HOW TO KEEP YOUR KIDS FROM DRIVING YOU CRAZY

HOW TO KEEP YOUR KIDS FROM DRIVING YOU CRAZY

A Proven Program for Improving Your Child's Behavior and Regaining Control of Your Family

Paula Stone Bender, Ph.D.

John Wiley & Sons, Inc.

New York • Chichester • Brisbane • Toronto • Singapore • Weinheim

Copyright © 1997 by Paula Stone Bender

Published by John Wiley & Sons, Inc.

Library of Congress Cataloging-in-Publication Data

Bender, Paula Stone.
    How to keep your kids from driving you crazy : a proven program for
  improving your child's behavior and regaining control of your family
  / Paula Stone Bender.
        p.   cm.
    Published simultaneously in Canada.
    ISBN 0–471–16888–2 (cloth : alk. paper). — ISBN 0–471–13012–5
  (pbk. : alk. paper)
    1. Child rearing.   2. Discipline of children.   I. Title.
  HQ769.B426   1997
  649'.64—dc20   96–20801

Printed in the United States of America

10 9 8 7 6 5 4 3 2 1

CONTENTS

PART TWO

BUILDING ON YOUR SUCCESS: CONTROLLING
PROBLEM BEHAVIOR, RAISING EXPECTATIONS,
AND IMPROVING COMMUNICATION

PART THREE
PERPETUATING A GOOD THING: KEEPING
THE GAME GOING AND UP-TO-DATE

ACKNOWLEDGMENTS

First and foremost I want to thank my children, Mike and Sean, and my husband, Bob, who, like it or not, served as ever-present guinea pigs as I developed and fine-tuned the Behavior Game in my home laboratory. My sister, Ann Stone, was always there as well, cheering me on and listening when I needed it most. Of course, special thanks go to my mom and dad, who in a positive and supportive way instilled in me the importance of behavior and its consequences from an early age.

The encouragement of my colleagues, especially my dear friend Paula Eastman, helped me persevere no matter what.

And without my agent, Joel Fishman, and my editor, Judith McCarthy, and her hardworking colleagues at John Wiley & Sons, Benjamin Hamilton, Chris Jackson, Glenn Morrison, and Elaine O'Neal, this book would never have taken its present form and been available to parents everywhere.

There are many others to thank and they know who they are, my many friends and colleagues who convinced me I could do it, to name just a few—John Hubner, Mary Itani Arredondo, Richard Beyer, Janet Burke, Hilda Kwok, Madelynn Rigopoulus, Joyce Smith, Debbie Glass, Marty Powell, Alice Snyder, Susan Phillips, Mary Jo Mock, and Carole Bardin.

A final thanks to all of those who have played the Game and shared their victories with me. The countless families I've worked with deserve a special round of applause and a heartfelt thank-you. Through thick and thin, they hung in there and showed me just how well the Game could work.

INTRODUCTION: KEEPING SANE WITH THE BEHAVIOR GAME

A re your children driving you crazy? Do you find yourself reminding them over and over to hurry up and do the everyday things they must, such as getting up and getting ready for school? Do they misbehave no matter what you do? In spite of your efforts, do they continue to disobey or whine or talk back? And even though you plead with them, is it still a struggle to get them to do their schoolwork and their chores? When they don't get what they want, do they throw temper tantrums or go to their room and sulk for hours? And what about your children getting along with each other? Is that the impossible dream? When you think about it, given the way they're acting, it's no wonder your kids are stressing you out.

Take heart, you're not alone. Kids will be kids. In fact, as you're reading this, children everywhere are driving their parents crazy just as they have been since the beginning of time. How come? Why does this keep happening? I think one reason is that parents rarely receive any preparation for the challenges of parenthood. Most jobs involve some kind of minimal training, but not parenting. You need to get a license before you're allowed to drive a car or get married, but, as everyone knows, no license is required to become a parent. With no prior experience, parents are expected to be successful at the most exhausting, unpredictable twenty-four-hour-a-day job there is—raising their children.

It's no wonder parents are confused and want help figuring out the right thing to do. That's where I come in. I'm a clinical psychologist who has spent twenty-five years working with families. A big part of my job is teaching

1

moms and dads how to be better parents. In my experience the best way to do this is to go beyond simply talking and to help parents take action at home. That's why I specialize in teaching parents techniques they can use to improve their child's behavior and help their family get along better. When I work with parents I show them how to combine love and discipline in positive and practical ways. I teach them how to create the supportive but structured environment their children need. I also encourage parents to solve problems that are just starting to happen, as well as those that have been going on for a long time.

Let me tell you, as I always do my clients, why I am so committed to an approach that empowers parents by teaching them how take action on their own to solve their children's problems and get problem behavior turned around. The best way to do this is for me to take you back to the time of my first client.

August 1969, Tucson, Arizona; Head Start program. Four-year-old Will was terrorizing his teachers and classmates. Out of control, his aggressive demeanor and salty language were sending shock waves throughout the school. Hoping to get some ideas about how to help Will, the principal contacted the psychology department at the University of Arizona. A psychology graduate student who was interested in working with children and families was asked to consult for this preschool program.

When naïve but well-meaning Ms. Stone (my maiden name) arrived for her first day on the job, reality hit hard and fast. Only moments after she came through the door the chaos was obvious. This was an open classroom where sixty preschoolers wandered from one learning center to another. Three teachers were assigned to control this mob and were doing an amazingly good job, with one exception: a feisty, unmanageable young boy named Will. Will was always acting up, commanding constant attention from the moment he arrived until the moment he left. He had mastered the art of getting what he wanted when he wanted it. He rarely sat still but instead seemed to move perpetually from place to place disrupting each table he passed.

All three teachers were quick to seek me out. With understandable desperation in their voices, they pleaded, "You've got to help us with Will. We don't know what to do with him. He's ruining everything."

Although I had no idea of what would work, I knew what wouldn't work. Like many young children, Will was not a good candidate for traditional therapy, play therapy, or any other kind of one-on-one talk therapy. He had made it very clear that he wasn't interested in talking to adults. His family was unavailable for counseling, so family therapy was ruled out as well. If Will was going to change, it was up to me and his teachers.

That evening I talked to everyone who would listen, then headed for the library in hopes of finding something I could try with Will. Reviewing the literature for relevant theories and research, I discovered a number of articles that described using "behavior modification techniques with children." These techniques were based on extensive scientific research concerning how children learn and behave. One of the earliest and most important "rules of learning" was that behavior that is rewarded tends to get stronger and happen again. In contrast, behavior that is not rewarded tends to get weaker and is less likely to be repeated. Therefore by controlling the kinds of consequences a child receives for certain behaviors, one can influence the kinds of behaviors a child displays. I decided that's what I'd try to do. I'd try to make sure that Will got rewards for his good behavior and discipline, such as a time-out, for his bad behavior.

Although skeptical, Will's teachers went along with my ideas about rewarding Will for good behavior, warning him once about problem behavior and then sending him to take a time-out (isolating him and leaving him alone for short periods of time). We picked rewards Will liked, little Matchbox cars and trucks, comic books, and inexpensive games. For good behavior Will would earn stars that would be put on a note card. If Will had earned enough stars during the day, he'd get to pick out a toy at the end of the day. Time-out would take place on a playground bench or in a corner of the classroom. We decided that I would try out these techniques with Will first to see if they'd work, and then if they did, his teachers would gradually take over. Will was not enthusiastic when I explained the reward system and time-out. But after a few trips to the isolation bench/corner and reminders about how he could earn stars and buy rewards, Will warmed up. Will became quite good at earning stars. After a while, he was rarely sent for a time-out because his behavior had improved so much. Perhaps most surprising, Will liked getting praise and encouragement from his teachers and Ms. Stone. Having learned how to get positive attention, Will no longer used his energy to get the negative attention he had craved before. Even now, as I remember Will I smile in appreciation; he taught me a lot and pointed me in the right direction.

After that I was hooked on working with children, parents, and families. As I saw more and more children and their parents, I realized that regardless of their child's particular problems, the parents with whom I was working would benefit greatly by learning how to use the kinds of techniques that I had used with Will. For example, if parents could learn how to reward their child for acting as the parents wanted, they would see an increase in these good behaviors. And if they could use discipline techniques like time-out consistently, they would be much better able to control their child's problem behaviors. My mission became clear: I would teach parents how to use these skills at home with their children. The seeds of my parent program I still use today were sown.

In the ensuing years, I developed my parenting program by translating psychologically sound, research-proven techniques into at-home projects parents could do with their children. (If you're interested in learning more about the theories and research findings that provided the basis for my program, I encourage you to refer to Appendix D for a list of books and articles on social learning theory and behavior therapy.)

Early on, I named my program the "Behavior Game." Like a traditional board game that you and your children play, there are rules and procedures, with choices, penalties, rewards and goals. And as you'll see later in this book, the Behavior Game has a simple, but vital, record-keeping system that allows "players" to "keep score" as they go—although this is a game that everyone playing can win. But most of all, my program for improving your children's behavior is a game because it is fun to play. Your kids will enjoy it, and you'll enjoy watching them act better and rewarding them for good behavior.

The Game took on a whole new wrinkle eighteen years ago when I myself had children. Since then, my two children have taught me the realities of parenting and showed me that the Game works when played on an hour-by-hour, day-by-day basis. Unlike my clients, my own children didn't leave after an hour of counseling. They were always there, no matter how busy or tired I was. My experience in the trenches as a parent helped me gain an appreciation for how difficult, exhausting, and time-consuming parenting is, as well as for what a good friend and big help the Behavior Game can be.

Over the years, the upside potential of the Behavior Game proved even greater than I anticipated. For more than two decades, I have taught my parenting program to hundreds of families as well as to professionals from the fields of pediatrics, psychiatry, psychology, social work, education, counsel-

ing, nursing, and community service. Today the program continues to flour-
ish. I find I'm always excited each time I invite a new parent to play the Behavior
Game.

On that note I'd like to invite you to join in and play the Game with your
children. Unfortunately, we won't have the chance to work together face to
face. However, I hope that this book will provide you with the information
and guidance you need to make the Game work. I like to think of myself as
being with you as you turn every page and take every step. If you're ready,
it's almost time to get started, but before you begin there are a few more things
I'd like to share.

First and foremost, I think it's wonderful that you care enough about your
children to want to help them and improve your parenting skills. They're lucky
kids to have parents who love them enough to take the time and effort any
parenting program (this one included) requires.

If you're feeling overwhelmed and/or skeptical about trying a parenting
program, let me reassure you that you're feeling as many other parents have
when they first encountered the Behavior Game. And, even if you feel there's
little you can do because it seems as if you've already tried everything, there's
still plenty of room for hope. With your effort and follow-through, my program can work for you and your family just as it has for hundreds of other
families.

In a nutshell, here's what you'll be doing. When you play the Game you'll
learn how to motivate your children to behave better from morning to night.
By providing rewards for good behaviors and discipline for problem behaviors, you'll help your child improve her behavior from the moment she gets
up until the time she goes to bed. You'll help her stop problem behaviors such
as tantrums, whining, disobedience and back talk. You'll encourage your child
to get along better with others, even her siblings. You'll develop a system with
incentives for studying and doing chores. And once you've conquered these
routine behaviors you'll be able to move on and help your child with more
complicated areas such as improving communication and assuming responsibility.

To make sure the Game works for you, I've tried to explain the "rules"
and "how to play" in an understandable and easy-to-follow manner. Each step
of the way, I outline exactly what you need to do, give you some pointers on
how to do it, and provide you with examples of how my clients did it. I provide specific instructions on how to try out the technique at home with your
kids. And to make sure I'm not wasting your time, I never ask you to do

anything unless it has been proven to work in scientific laboratories and in home laboratories, mine included.

As you begin this journey, I'll ask you the same favors I do of every other parent: Please start out with a positive outlook and open mind. Even if you've tried programs before and they didn't work, I want you to envision what you're going to be doing as an exciting, challenging journey, not a series of dreaded tasks. Done in the right spirit, the Behavior Game is a fun experience for the whole family, especially your children.

Even though you may be in a hurry, take your time and learn how to put each new parenting technique into action before moving on to the next one. Experience has taught me the importance of learning the art of rewarding first before trying out anything else. Therefore, I strongly recommend that you follow the order specified in this book. If you go out of order and try out discipline techniques first, in the long run, you will slow yourself down and cause problems.

And since this book will serve as your official source for the Behavior Game, please spend the next few moments getting acquainted with how to use it to full advantage.

HOW TO USE THIS BOOK

This book is a guide for parents with children from the ages of two through twelve. The Behavior Game is most effective when played with toddler to preteen children. At each age level the Game can help your children master the developmental and transitional challenges they're facing, whether it's adjusting to preschool, sharing with friends, welcoming a new sibling, entering elementary school, living with a single parent, getting braces or glasses, accepting a stepparent, coping with both parents working, moving to a new town, doing school work, following through on chores, accepting new responsibilities, or getting along with the family. Although the guidelines presented in this book can work for teenagers, many thirteen- and fourteen-year-olds are less than enthusiastic about playing a game and having a chart, so the best time to get the Behavior Game started is before your child becomes a teenager. The Game can be used successfully by both large and small families. You can play the Game with one or all of your children; however, most parents find that it works best to involve all their preteen children.

Both two-parent and single-parent households can play. If you live in a two-parent household and both parents want to be involved, that's great. If one parent wants to take the lead, that's okay too. Choose whatever arrangement is best for your family, and remember that the Game will work better if you're willing to compromise and be flexible. Parents often find that an open mind and time to discuss what they're doing makes things go more smoothly. If you head a single-parent household, you may want to find a supportive "buddy" who can listen and help you over any rough patches you encounter as you play the Game.

Since the Game is for both boys and girls, you'll notice that throughout the book I've alternated using male and female pronouns and adjectives. All references to "he" or "she" apply to both boys and girls. Also note that when I use the word *child*, it applies to one or more children.

This book is divided into three main parts. The first part explains how to define and encourage good behaviors, thus establishing a foundation for success. Chapters 1 through 4 detail how to set up the Behavior Game and begin playing. Part Two describes how to build on your initial success. Chapter 5 explains how to use the Game to control problem behaviors. Chapter 6 talks about raising expectations for your child's behavior and including in the Game other adults who care for your child. Finally, Part Three describes how to perpetuate your success with details on keeping the Game going and up-to-date.

I can't stress enough that you must "play the Game" in the order presented. No matter how much your kids are driving you crazy, resist the temptation to leap ahead to chapter 5 on discipline. The Game will work only if you first establish good behaviors for your children and put in place a system for encouraging them through rewards. My techniques are based on over twenty-five years of experience helping hundreds of parents cope with one of life's most difficult, but satisfying, jobs—raising kids.

Think of the Behavior Game as a valuable tool for fulfilling the long-term commitment of parenting. Although you should see improvement in your child's behavior in a week or so, because they will be enthusiastic about playing, the Game is an ongoing process, not a quick fix. You'll stay with Part One for a *few weeks* before expanding the Game and raising standards of behavior in Part Two. After six to eight weeks with the Game, consult Part Three for how to take stock and how to adapt the Game for *years* of success in the future.

Of course, over time you should read the whole book at whatever pace suits you. If you are able to spend a few minutes every day learning about the Behavior Game, it will begin to become part of your routine, just as it will when you play it with your children.

As you read through the book, you'll be asked to do a series of projects. It's very important that you do these projects. Just reading about them won't work. To help out, I've included case studies on how my clients played the Game with their children (names and specific identifying information changed, of course). Most projects ask you to fill out a checklist or chart. I've provided samples of the checklists and charts in the text, and in Appendix A, you'll find blank forms to copy and use. I'll highlight these tasks in boxed "To Do" instructions in the chapters. In general, your participation requires defining good behaviors for your kids and recording when they do them. You'll find that it's less tedious, and more rewarding, than you might have thought at first.

Keep in mind that most of my clients are pleasantly surprised by how well the Game works and how much their children like to play it. Many families I work with refer to the Game as an exciting and rewarding journey. As you follow each step of this book, I hope you find your trip a pleasant and successful one as well. Good luck to you and your family as you embark on your mission *possible*.

As a final note, your experience with the Game is important to me. Your feedback will help me make the Game even better and more effective. So, if you get the chance, please share what happened when you and your child played the Game by writing to me, Paula Stone Bender, Ph.D., c/o John Wiley and Sons, Inc., 605 Third Avenue, New York, NY, 10158-0012.

PART ONE

ENCOURAGING GOOD BEHAVIOR BY PLAYING THE BEHAVIOR GAME

1

GETTING READY TO PLAY
THE BEHAVIOR GAME

If your children are driving you crazy, the Behavior Game is just what your family needs. This Game rewards your children for doing what you want them to and discourages them from doing things you don't want them to. It is the result of my twenty-five years of experience helping hundreds of moms and dads become better parents. Within the specific guidelines I'll give you, you'll define the rules of the Game to fit your family's special needs. After playing the Game for even a week or two, you will see considerable improvement in your child's behavior.

First you need to lay some groundwork for playing the Game. This chapter will get you ready by teaching you the fundamentals, including how the Game can help, why watching good behavior is so important, and how to use rewards to get your child to behave better.

HOW THE GAME CAN HELP YOUR CHILD

The goal of the Behavior Game is to help your entire family get along better the whole day, every day. The Game makes it more likely that your child will do what you want her to, such as cooperating, sharing, doing chores, completing homework, and being nice. It also makes it less likely that she'll do the things you don't want her to, such as disobeying, talking back, and fighting.

You'll find that as your family plays the Behavior Game and your child's behavior improves, a lot of other good things happen too—attitudes get better, feelings become more positive, and your family has more fun together.

11

The Game is structured so that you and your children work as a team. You, the parent or parents, are the team leaders who oversee the Game and make certain that it's working.

What Problems Can the Behavior Game Help You Solve?

Let's take a look at some of the problems the Behavior Game has helped other families solve. As you read over these problems, put a check by each one that occurs in your family.

- ☐ In the morning my child has a tough time getting out of bed. I usually have to ask him repeatedly to get up.
- ☐ We're always rushed in the morning and no one is ever ready for school on time.
- ☐ Mealtimes are often unpleasant because my child either refuses to eat or plays around and misbehaves.
- ☐ My children argue and tease one another too much.
- ☐ Sometimes my child just can't get her homework done.
- ☐ My child rarely minds me or does what I ask.
- ☐ It seems as if my child doesn't listen whenever I say something she doesn't want to hear.
- ☐ My child rarely does her chores unless I ask her repeatedly.
- ☐ Sometimes it seems as if the family just can't get along and all we do is argue and yell.
- ☐ My child talks back to me sometimes and I wonder if he respects me.
- ☐ When my child gets angry, she often throws a temper tantrum.
- ☐ Getting my child to bed is usually a struggle.

These kinds of problems happen in most families. What about yours? If you're like most parents, you want the problems you checked to go away.

Well, you're in luck. The Behavior Game can help you solve these problems. It can help your children improve their behavior from the time they get up in the morning until the time they go to bed at night.

As I work with clients, I find it always helps for them to be able to follow along and see someone else play the Game. That's why I created the Bradley family. The Bradley family's experiences are based on the experiences of many different families who have come to me for help. Finding out how they complete each chapter will make your job much easier. Let's take a minute to meet the Bradleys and find out why they came to me for help.

From our first meeting it was obvious that Joan and Gary Bradley wanted to be good parents to their children, nine-year-old Cindy and six-year-old Bobby. But no matter how hard they tried, everyone was always arguing, and no one could get along with anyone else. Finally, after they'd had a huge fight with Cindy, Joan and Gary came to me for advice.

Cindy's best friend, Ellen, had gotten a new bike, and Cindy desperately wanted to see it right away. She couldn't believe her mom would say, "Not now. You'll have to wait until after dinner." Ellen's house was only next door. Ellen was her best friend, and Cindy wanted to be the first person to see Ellen's new bike. So, as usual, Cindy refused to take "no" for an answer.

Cindy started working on her mother as only Cindy could. "It isn't like I'm asking for a new bike myself. I don't complain that I have that old, beat-up bike with the tires that go flat all the time. All I want is to be the first person to see the bike. That's all. I'll eat dinner when I get back. I won't be there long. Please, Mom! You never let me do anything I want. I just want to go for five minutes. Please let me go." And then, of course, Cindy started crying. Knowing that a big fight was only moments away, Bobby fled to his room, closed his door, and turned on his favorite video game.

Joan couldn't take Cindy's ranting and raving any longer. She wanted her gone. Joan screamed back, "All right go to Ellen's, but you'd better be back by dinnertime."

Joan was fuming. Why had she given in to Cindy again? Why did Cindy act this way? Why couldn't Joan reason with Cindy? Joan felt that she'd lost control, and it didn't feel good. Before things got any worse, Joan knew she needed to get some help.

After listening to Joan and Gary, I recommended that the whole family get started playing the Behavior Game as soon as possible.

Where Should You Start?

Thinking about trying to change the problems your family is having can be overwhelming and confusing. Where do you start? What should you do first?

If you're like most parents, you've probably already tried everything you could think of to make things better. Most parents repeatedly make a serious, heartfelt effort to be more understanding, encouraging, and support-ive of their children. They promise themselves that they won't get angry as often and that they'll remain calm and patient no matter what happens. But even though they're sincere when they make these promises, they usually can't keep them, at least not for very long. You've probably met with the same frustrations.

Why is it so hard to be the kind of parent you want to be? Why is it so difficult to be more patient, understanding, and supportive with your chil-dren? One important reason is your children's behavior.

You can't be the kind of parent you want to be unless your child's behav-ior improves. Most of the parents I work with truly want to be better parents, but no matter how hard they try, they can't until their child begins being more cooperative. Let's look in on my session with Joan and Gary Bradley as they describe their efforts to bring peace to their family.

Before they learned about the Behavior Game, Joan and Gary told me that they often used a weekly pep talk to encourage everyone to get along better. Cindy and Bobby never failed to nod and promise to be good. But as every parent knows, making promises and keeping them are two different things.

On a recent Monday morning, Joan was determined to start off the week on the right note. She cheerfully reminded Cindy and Bobby that it was time to get up and get ready for school. As usual her efforts were met with silence, and Joan found herself nagging them to hurry up and get ready. By the time Cindy and Bobby came to breakfast she was fuming inside but somehow managed to keep her cool as they all piled into the car and left for school. As Joan thought about the morning she realized she was angry and disappointed; she'd kept her part of the bargain, she'd been nice and understanding. Why had her children behaved so poorly? What was wrong with them?

As the day wore on Joan tried to forget about the morning and concen-trate on starting over and making the afternoon better. When the children got home she reminded them of their promise to help the family get along. This reminder seemed to work for about fifteen minutes, until Cindy and Bobby got into a fight over who got the last cookie. Hiding her frustration,

Joan nicely told each of them to go straighten up their rooms. Although both went to their rooms, neither did any cleaning. Cindy played with her dolls and Bobby played a video game. Joan felt defeated. She'd tried and failed. Maybe Gary could do better when he got home. Not surprisingly, Gary wasn't any more effective than Joan. Only after threatening to take away television privileges forever was Gary finally able to get Cindy and Bobby to go to bed. Joan and Gary were exhausted, depressed, and upset. Their plan was a total failure.

Days like this happen in the lives of many parents. Parents who really want to be positive, upbeat, supportive, and understanding find that they can't be when their children misbehave repeatedly. No matter how hard they try, eventually their attempts to be calm and understanding fail as their children's behavior gets increasingly worse.

Maybe you, too, have had days like the one you just read about. If you have, you know how frustrating it is to try to be the kind of parent you want to be when your child is misbehaving.

Unfortunately, there is no quick fix, but there are steps you can take to turn things around. As a first step to breaking the cycle of misbehavior, I recommend that you spend a few days carefully watching your child. Even though you may spend a lot of time with your child and feel that you're aware of everything she does, it's still a good idea to take some extra time and focus on her behavior, *especially her good behavior.*

Once you know exactly what your child is doing, you'll be able to decide what behaviors you want her to change. As you watch your child, use this general guideline to decide whether a behavior is good and you want to keep it or if it's a problem and you want to change it: If you like your child's behavior and want it to continue, it's probably good; if you don't like your child's behavior and want it to stop, it's probably a problem behavior.

Most parents like to see their child get up, get ready, and leave for school without a hassle. They're also pleased when their child treats other family members nicely, does what is asked, finishes chores, and does schoolwork. In addition, they're happy when their child gets ready for bed and goes to bed on time.

On the other hand, when children do the opposite of any of these good behaviors, parents are rarely pleased. Parents don't like to have their children refuse to get up or go to bed, argue and talk back, or disobey them.

PAYING EXTRA ATTENTION
TO GOOD BEHAVIOR

In some families, parents become so concerned about their children's problem behavior that they stop noticing when their children behave well. If this has happened to you, you need to break this habit by concentrating on what you like about the way your child behaves. Later on there will be time to deal directly with what they do that drives you crazy. But for now, look very carefully for behavior you want to encourage.

Many parents are surprised when I urge them to "tune out the bad and tune in the good." For many clients this positive focus clashes with their long-standing belief that the best way to get rid of problem behavior is to concentrate on it and choose the best punishments to deal with it. But my twenty-five years as a clinical psychologist have taught me that nothing could be further from the truth.

The Behavior Game begins by focusing on good behavior because in order to encourage your child's good behavior, you need to find out just what that is. Only after good behavior is established—usually after a few weeks—*only then* can you move on to tackling problem behavior.

As you look for good behavior, here are some guidelines to follow:

•   **For behavior to be good, it doesn't have to be perfect.**   Many parents are surprised to learn that good behavior doesn't mean perfect behavior. Good behavior doesn't mean that when your child cleans up her room every toy and piece of clothing is put away "just right." Instead, it means she tries and does a little better each time. Good behavior doesn't mean that your child gets all As on her report card; instead, it means she tries hard and does her schoolwork. When your child puts forth some effort and tries, that's good behavior.

•   **For behavior to be good, it doesn't have to last a long time.**   If your children play nicely with each other for five minutes, that's five minutes of good behavior. If your child works on her schoolwork for fifteen minutes, that's fifteen minutes of good behavior. Short periods of good behavior are still good behavior.

•   **For behavior to be good, it doesn't have to happen all the time.**   Good behaviors that only happen sometimes, or even rarely, are still good behaviors. Even if your child talks back to you most of the time, when she talks nicely to you, that's good behavior no matter how infrequently it happens. If every once in a while your daughter goes to bed on time, that's good behavior.

•   **Good behavior can be fairly quiet and easy to ignore.**   Behavior such as getting along, studying quietly, or getting ready for school without complaining may not get your attention as easily as behavior such as arguing, yelling, and whining. Too often parents ignore these quiet examples of good behavior. Try to spend extra time looking for hard-to-notice good behavior.

When you're looking for good behavior, pay special attention to the things listed below. This list will help ensure that you don't miss any of your child's good behavior.

•   **Getting up on time.**   Getting up on time when asked or when the alarm clock rings, not complaining or making excuses.

•   **Getting dressed without a hassle.**   Getting dressed when asked, not making a fuss about clothes, and not taking too long.

•   **Taking care of self.**   Taking care of oneself by brushing teeth, washing face, combing hair, and whatever else needs to be done.

•   **Eating breakfast nicely.**   Coming to breakfast on time, sitting at the table, eating at least a few bites, not taking too long, and being pleasant.

•   **Being ready for school.**   Being ready to leave for school on time: having backpack packed, lunch made, jacket on, and whatever else has to be done.

•   **Getting along with brothers or sisters.**   Doing something together nicely without fighting, yelling, or name-calling: sharing, helping each other, cooperating, and playing together.

•   **Getting along with friends.**   Playing nicely with friends.

•   **Getting along with Mom or Dad.**   Having a nice time doing something with Mom or Dad, talking pleasantly, answering questions when asked and not arguing.

•   **Doing what is asked.**   Performing a task, now not later, without being asked many times and without arguing.

•   **Doing chores.**   Completing chores around the house without a hassle and without being reminded more than one time.

•   **Doing schoolwork.**   Paying attention and concentrating on a task, usually school related. Younger children may color or put a puzzle together; older children may finish a homework assignment or study for a test.

•   **Eating dinner nicely.**   Coming to the dinner table when called, sitting without jumping up, eating at least a few bites of food, and talking in a pleasant, civil manner.

• **Getting ready for bed on time.** Doing whatever needs to get done in order to be ready for bed, such as brushing teeth, going to the bathroom, washing face, taking a bath, and putting on pajamas, and doing these in a timely manner.

• **Going to bed on time.** Being in bed, lying down with head on pillow, at the appropriate time.

• **Staying in bed.** Staying in bed and not getting out of bed until the next morning except in emergencies.

After you've watched for your child's good behavior for a few days, you'll be rating these examples for each of your children who is playing the Game. To help you do this I developed the Good Behavior Checklist. (Please see sample on the following page.)

As you can see from the sample, you'll be rating how frequently each of your child's good behaviors happens.

Before you begin this project, let's look in on the Bradleys as they fill out Cindy's and Bobby's checklists.

After spending several days watching their children's good behavior, Joan and Gary were surprised by what they saw. Cindy behaved better than they expected, while Bobby was worse. It also became clear that they didn't always agree on how to rate their children's behavior. However, by working together and talking things over they were able to finish a checklist for each child.

As they looked over their completed checklists, they realized that the behavior they saw as happening "often" or "sometimes," such as eating breakfast and dinner nicely, being ready for school on time, getting along with friends, and staying in bed would be much easier to work with than the behavior that they "rarely" or "never" saw. The good behavior that rarely occurred included getting up on time, getting along with each other, doing chores, doing schoolwork, getting ready for bed, and going to bed. Getting this behavior to occur more often would definitely be a challenge.

Although they realized they had their work cut out for them, Joan and Gary didn't feel as hopeless as they had at first. As they looked at their checklists, it was clear that both Cindy and Bobby behaved well some of the time. They agreed that at least they had a starting point. (See sample checklists for Cindy and Bobby on the following pages.)

Good Behavior Checklist

For _____

Instructions: Indicate whether your child displays each kind of behavior "often," "sometimes," "rarely," or "never." If you're not sure how frequently a particular kind of behavior occurs, spend a few more days watching your child.

MORNING BEHAVIOR	OFTEN	SOMETIMES	RARELY	NEVER
Getting up on time				
Getting dressed without a hassle				
Taking care of self				
Eating breakfast nicely				
Being ready for school				
Other				

DAILY BEHAVIOR	OFTEN	SOMETIMES	RARELY	NEVER
Getting along with brothers or sisters				
Getting along with friends				
Getting along with Mom or Dad				
Doing what is asked				
Doing chores				
Doing schoolwork				
Eating dinner nicely				
Other				

BEDTIME BEHAVIOR	OFTEN	SOMETIMES	RARELY	NEVER
Getting ready for bed on time				
Going to bed on time				
Staying in bed				
Other				

Good Behavior Checklist

For *Cindy Bradley*

Instructions: Indicate whether your child displays each kind of behavior "often," "sometimes," "rarely," or "never." If you're not sure how frequently a particular kind of behavior occurs, spend a few more days watching your child.

MORNING BEHAVIOR	OFTEN	SOMETIMES	RARELY	NEVER
Getting up on time			✔	
Getting dressed without a hassle	✔			
Taking care of self	✔			
Eating breakfast nicely		✔		
Being ready for school		✔		
Other				

DAILY BEHAVIOR	OFTEN	SOMETIMES	RARELY	NEVER
Getting along with brothers or sisters			✔	
Getting along with friends		✔		
Getting along with Mom or Dad		✔ (Dad)	✔ (Mom)	
Doing what is asked			✔	
Doing chores			✔	
Doing schoolwork			✔	
Eating dinner nicely		✔		
Other *feeding Freckles*	✔			

BEDTIME BEHAVIOR	OFTEN	SOMETIMES	RARELY	NEVER
Getting ready for bed on time			✔	
Going to bed on time			✔	
Staying in bed	✔			
Other				

Good Behavior Checklist

For _Bobby Bradley_

Instructions: Indicate whether your child displays each kind of behavior "often," "sometimes," "rarely," or "never." If you're not sure how frequently a particular kind of behavior occurs, spend a few more days watching your child.

MORNING BEHAVIOR	OFTEN	SOMETIMES	RARELY	NEVER
Getting up on time			✓	
Getting dressed without a hassle			✓	
Taking care of self			✓	
Eating breakfast nicely		✓		
Being ready for school		✓		
Other				

DAILY BEHAVIOR	OFTEN	SOMETIMES	RARELY	NEVER
Getting along with brothers or sisters			✓	
Getting along with friends		✓		
Getting along with Mom or Dad		✓		
Doing what is asked		✓		
Doing chores			✓	
Doing schoolwork			✓	
Eating dinner nicely		✓		
Other				

BEDTIME BEHAVIOR	OFTEN	SOMETIMES	RARELY	NEVER
Getting ready for bed on time			✓	
Going to bed on time			✓	
Staying in bed		✓		
Other				

Joan and Gary's revelation was not unusual. Over the years, many of my clients have been surprised to see that their children were sometimes good. I'm sure that as you fill out a Good Behavior Checklist for your child, you'll discover your child behaves well some of the time.

To Do

1. *Copy:* For each child who will be playing, make a copy of the Good Behavior Checklist, which you'll find in Appendix A.
2. *Fill out:* Based on the good behavior you've seen for the past several days, fill out a checklist for each child.
3. *Save:* Put your checklist in a safe, easy-to-find place. You'll need to review it later.

After you've filled out your checklist, take a moment to review it. Overall, how did your child do? Don't worry if you didn't see very much good behavior. No matter how infrequently your child behaves well now, as you play the Behavior Game you'll see better behavior increasingly often.

Next you'll find out about rewards and how to use them with your child.

LEARNING ABOUT REWARDS

Be sure to spend enough time on this section so that you thoroughly understand what rewards are and how to use them correctly. Without this information you won't be able to play the Behavior Game successfully.

What Are Rewards?

Rewards are the heart and soul of the Behavior Game. Quite simply, without rewards the Game won't work. Remember, you need to reward your child's good behavior if you want the Behavior Game to bring about the changes you're hoping for.

Some of the parents I work with resist the idea of rewards at first, thinking that they shouldn't have to "bribe" their children for good behavior. It's important to understand that rewards and bribes are different. Rewards are used as *positive incentives* that your child *earns* for behaving well. When you use rewards you plan ahead. You and your child know exactly how your reward system works. On the other hand, bribes are inducements used to get someone to do something he thinks is wrong or that he doesn't want to do. For example, when parents ask their child to lie about something in exchange for a favor, that's a bribe. If a parent gives a child money in exchange for keeping quiet, that's a bribe as well. Bribes tend to be unplanned, poorly reasoned inducements that are not in the best interest of the child, because they encourage him to do something he shouldn't. In contrast, when used as part of the Behavior Game, rewards are planned, systematically used incentives that help children improve and behave better.

As you think about rewards, keep these tips in mind:

• **Rewards can be anything your child likes.**   Rewards can be something your child likes to do or something she likes to have or something she likes to hear. They can be activities, things, or words of praise and encouragement.

• **Many different kinds of activities can be rewards to your child.**   Your child may like free time when he can pick a favorite activity such as watching television, playing a game, listening to music, reading a story, or doing an art project. He may also enjoy being with friends.

• **Many different kinds of things can be rewards to your child.**   Just like adults, children like to have "stuff," whether they'd like a toy, a ball, a doll, a sticker, a music tape, or a video game. Your child probably has a list of the things he'd like to have. So long as what he wants is reasonable and inexpensive, it's a good reward.

• **Different children can like different things.**   What is a reward to one child may be a kind of punishment to another. Your daughter may like to play soccer, while your son may not. Your son may love to go to the arcade to play video games, but your daughter may hate it. Preferences may vary as well. One child may choose vanilla ice cream, while another may choose chocolate.

• **The age of your child can also affect what rewards she likes.**   A two-year-old may like getting stickers, while a ten-year-old may love collecting baseball cards. A five-year-old may think going on a walk with you is great, while a twelve-year-old would rather talk to friends on the phone. A six-year-old may do almost anything to get the chance to play a video game, while a three-year-old would rather play with blocks.

• **Many different kinds of words, especially your words of praise and encouragement, can be rewards to your child.**   Giving verbal rewards can be difficult for many parents, either because they find the (often unaccustomed) process awkward or because they object to praising what they believe should be "expected" behavior. My answers to these concerns are that practice will make you more comfortable giving verbal praise (and you'll enjoy your child's response), and "expected" behavior is something children learn a little at a time. Through the Behavior Game's system of positive rewards, you are in fact teaching them in a manner far more effective than simply telling them.

Indeed, without your kind words of support the Game won't work very well. The Behavior Game depends on parents using their words to communicate their praise, encouragement, recognition, and support to their children. Hearing positive things and getting their parents' praise and attention is rewarding for children. They like knowing that you noticed when they did a good job or when they tried hard. (See the following section for some help on how to deliver verbal rewards.)

Whenever you use words to express positive feelings you are giving a reward. When you say, "That really meant a lot to me. Thank you," you're giving a reward. When you give praise and pay attention to your child you're rewarding him. When you say, "I liked that," or "Thanks for doing that," you're giving rewards with your words.

• **Probably the two most important rewards in the Behavior Game are your time and attention.**   Children want to spend fun time with their parents, time without arguing, time when they're listened to and when they receive their parents' full attention.

Don't worry if rewards haven't worked before. If used in the context of the Game, they will work. But you need to know the right time and the right way to give rewards.

When to Give Rewards

To increase good behavior, give the reward *after* it happens, never before. Rewards should be used as positive consequences for good behavior, not for the promise of it. When used as positive consequences, rewards will teach your children to behave well more often. The consequences children receive for their behavior determine how they will act in the future. So, if a child is rewarded for a certain kind of behavior, she will display that behavior more often.

Although using rewards may sound easy, it's never as simple as most parents hope it will be. To help make giving rewards easier, we'll look at how the Bradleys initially used rewards. As you read, think about whether Joan followed the guidelines discussed above and ask yourself how she could have used rewards differently to get her son's behavior to change.

Joan desperately wanted her son Bobby to show more responsibility and learn how to clean his bedroom. Tired of arguing about this problem and getting nowhere, Joan decided to try using rewards in an attempt to get Bobby to clean his room.

As a reward for cleaning his room, Joan offered Bobby a picture book he wanted. Bobby promised to clean his room, but he begged his mom to let him look at his new book for just a few minutes before he got started. Joan was hesitant about this idea but let Bobby see the book "just for five minutes" because, after all, he had promised to clean his room.

Although Joan asked Bobby repeatedly to clean his room, he never got around to it. He meant to clean his room, but his new book was so interesting that he spent most of the evening looking at it. Even after Joan took the book away, he didn't clean his room. Joan was frustrated and confused because she'd used a reward but it hadn't worked.

Why didn't Joan's reward work with Bobby? What guideline didn't Joan follow? Joan didn't give Bobby the reward *after* he had behaved well; instead, she gave it to him before he performed his part of the deal by cleaning his room.

In the future if Joan wants rewards to work, no matter how much he begs, Joan needs to wait and give Bobby his reward after he cleans his room. Let's find out about some other important guidelines you need to follow when using rewards.

How to Give Rewards

Not only does it matter when you give rewards, how you give them is also important. Here are some guidelines:

- **Give your child advance notice of when good behavior is expected.** Rewards work best if children know ahead of time what kinds of good behavior you plan to reward. Whenever possible, let your child know in advance about what you expect. For example, if you plan to reward him for studying, let him know that in five minutes it will be time to start studying. This preparation helps everyone get in the right mood and gives your child a chance to get ready to do what you want.
- **Use frequent reminders of what the good behavior entails.** You should also use specific reminders that let your child know exactly what she needs to do to earn a reward. For example, instead of saying, "Clean your room," describe exactly what you mean. Does she need to put her toys away, make her bed, put her dirty clothes in the hamper? Is there anything else she needs to do? The more your child knows about what you expect and how you plan to reward her, the better the rewards will work.
- **Use specific words of praise.** After your child followed your instructions and behaved accordingly, let him know how much you like what he did. Be specific. Mention each good thing he did. Let your child know exactly what you like and what you're rewarding.
- **Provide encouragement and help when needed.** Help your child earn a reward by assisting her with tasks she can't do by herself. If she needs your help getting ready in the morning, make sure she gets it. If she's having trouble with chores or schoolwork and needs your help, make sure you give it to her.
- **Be pleasant, enthusiastic, and positive.** Give your attention, praise, and encouragement when your child behaves well. Let your child know that you're pleased. *Be yourself but be positive and upbeat.* Whether you're rewarding accomplishment or your child's attempts to display good behavior, make sure he knows that you appreciate his efforts.
- **Reward as quickly as possible.** Give your child a reward as soon as you can after her good behavior. This linkage is especially important for younger children.
- **Don't use criticism and rewards together.** Rewards lose their effectiveness when they're combined with criticism. If you feel you need to correct your child, wait a while. Don't correct him right after you've told him what a good job he's done. For example, don't thank him for cleaning up the kitchen and then tell him that he could have done a better job; don't say something like, "That's a good job on your spelling paper but look at how messy it is," or "Thanks for helping with dinner, now clean that filthy room of yours." Thank your child and leave it at that. You can correct him later.

- **Reward behavior that is happening now.**   Plan to reward your child's good behavior now; don't reward the good behavior you wish she would display. Make it easy, not hard, to earn rewards. Reward effort and small improvements, not perfection.
- **Keep rewarding.**   It takes more than one or two rewards to change behavior. You need to continue to give rewards if you want behavior to change.

It's very important to follow all of these guidelines if you want rewards to work. Since there are so many guidelines it usually takes a while to learn to use all of them together. Let's look in again on Joan Bradley as she tries one more time to use rewards to get her son Bobby to clean his room.

This time Joan vowed not to make the same mistake—Bobby wouldn't get his reward until after he cleaned his room. Since Bobby had started showing some interest in earning a little money, Joan decided he could earn a quarter if he cleaned his room.

In a hurry to get the laundry started, Joan asked Bobby to clean his room, "Bobby, just this once, do you think it would be too much to ask you to clean your room while I'm doing the laundry? I'll even give you a quarter." The money sounded good, so Bobby agreed. As he was putting his toys in the toy box, Bobby realized this wasn't so bad; in fact, maybe he could do more stuff like this and get more and more money. After he was finished putting his toys away, he didn't know what to do next. When he called his mom for help, she shouted back that she'd be there as soon as she could. Tired of waiting and still confused about what to do next, Bobby started looking through his new picture book.

When Joan finally came to Bobby's room and found him looking at a book, she was furious. How typical, she thought. What a mess. Bobby never finishes anything. "Well, young man," Joan growled at Bobby, "I guess you can't even do something simple like cleaning your room. You're not getting a penny for this awful job."

Bobby was confused; he'd tried and now he was getting punished. "But Mom," Bobby pleaded, "I was just waiting for you to tell me what else I needed to do and how to do it."

Why didn't Joan's reward work? What did she do wrong? For starters, she wasn't very pleasant when she asked Bobby to clean his room. She didn't let him know specifically what she wanted him to do. She wasn't responsive when Bobby called her for some help and encouragement. She didn't notice the good things Bobby had done; she noticed only what Bobby hadn't done. She didn't praise Bobby for what he had done, and she didn't give him the reward she had promised him.

In the future if Joan wants rewards to work she should be pleasant and enthusiastic, saying something like, "It would sure help me out if you could clean your room. I'll give you a quarter for trying." She should be specific. She should tell Bobby exactly what she wants him to do, and if necessary she should show him how to perform the different tasks. She should come as soon as she can if Bobby calls her for help. If she can't come right away because she's doing something she can't stop, such as cooking dinner or talking on the phone, she should explain this to Bobby. And, instead of expecting perfection, she should look for the good things Bobby has done and praise him for doing them.

Being Positive While Giving Rewards

When the time comes for giving rewards, you'll need to be positive and upbeat. So, why not start developing the habit of being positive right now? Take a moment and ask yourself the following questions about how you already act with your children.

What kinds of words and actions do I use with my children? Do I smile and laugh with them? Am I pleasant and supportive, or do I tend to be critical and discouraging? Do I tell my children when they do things that I like, or do I let them know how I feel only when they've done something wrong? Do I use humor with my children and try to enjoy being with them?

If you don't tend to be positive and upbeat, take heart, you can change. Here are some ideas about how to become a more positive parent.

• **Acknowledge good behavior and don't expect perfection.** For example, if you ask your son to make his bed and he tries, praise him for trying and doing what you asked him to do. Even if the bedspread is wrinkled and lumpy and hanging over one side too much, don't criticize him for not doing a perfect job. Let him know you appreciate his efforts.

Hold your tongue when you want to correct your child for something that isn't really important or that he isn't doing "just right." For example, if your child is working on his spelling words don't criticize his handwriting or neatness. Praise him for the words he knows and encourage him to learn the ones he doesn't. Again, remember that whenever your child is helping you, you need to acknowledge his efforts.

• **Practice saying nice things.** Practice smiling and saying the nice things you want to say. Some parents find it helpful to look in the mirror when they're practicing what they want to say, whether it's, "Thanks for your help!" or "I can see you really tried," or "It makes me feel good to see you helping," or "You are a good helper today!" or "Good for you! You're trying!" Even though this may feel funny, do it anyway. Practice will pay off in the future. Don't be shy; you've done sillier things in your life.

• **Say at least one positive thing to each family member each day.** Try to start the day by giving everyone a positive comment. If this doesn't work, don't give up—you'll have other chances in the afternoon and evening to say something nice. It can take a while to develop the habit of being pleasant and positive. For some parents it's easier than for others. If you have to work at it, don't worry. It will happen.

Now that you know what rewards are, you can begin deciding which rewards you want to use with your child.

CHOOSING REWARDS FOR YOUR CHILD'S BEHAVIOR GAME

To help choose the rewards to use with your child, review the list of rewards that has been used successfully by many families I have worked with. This list appears on the Reward Checklist on the next page. You'll be filling one out for each of your children who is playing the Game.

As you can see from the sample, you'll be picking from three different groups: daily rewards, weekly rewards, and monthly rewards. First of all, your Game must include rewards your child can earn every day. In fact, your child needs to be able to look forward to earning at least *several* daily rewards. Waiting all week to get a reward is too long. Your child will lose her motivation to change. However, most children also look forward to one or two weekly rewards that they can enjoy on the weekend. And some older children like bigger monthly rewards they can look forward to.

Reward Checklist

For _____

Instructions: Check each reward that you want to include in your child's Behavior Game.

DAILY REWARDS

15 minutes of free time

- ☐ Be with Mom or Dad
- ☐ Read a story
- ☐ Play a game
- ☐ Go for a walk
- ☐ Play with toys
- ☐ Watch television
- ☐ Listen to music
- ☐ Talk on telephone

Other fun things

- ☐ _____
- ☐ _____
- ☐ _____

Food treat

- ☐ _____
- ☐ _____

Being with friends

- ☐ Have a friend over
- ☐ Visit a friend
- ☐ Other _____

Bedtime rewards

- ☐ Extra bedtime story
- ☐ Stay up 30 minutes later
- ☐ Other _____

Earning money

- ☐ For good behaviors

Other rewards

- ☐ _____
- ☐ _____

WEEKLY REWARDS

Weekend activities

- ☐ With Mom or Dad
- ☐ With friends
- ☐ See a movie
- ☐ Go out to lunch
- ☐ Have a friend overnight
- ☐ Go to a friend's house

Other fun things

- ☐ _____
- ☐ _____
- ☐ _____

Getting something new

- ☐ An affordable toy/game/book
- ☐ Rent a game or video
- ☐ Sports item
- ☐ Clothes, stuff to wear

Other new stuff to get

- ☐ _____
- ☐ _____
- ☐ _____

MONTHLY REWARDS

Saving up for

- ☐ _____
- ☐ _____

Other rewards

- ☐ _____
- ☐ _____

As you're reading about each of the following rewards, ask yourself if you would feel comfortable including it as part of your child's Behavior Game. Don't include any rewards that you feel are inappropriate. Don't include any rewards you feel are too big or too difficult to give. Pick only those rewards that feel right for you and your child.

To Do

1. *Copy:* For each child who's playing the Game, make a copy of the Reward Checklist, which you'll find in Appendix A.
2. *Fill out:* As you fill out a Reward Checklist for each child, review the following sections on daily, weekly, and monthly rewards.
3. *Save:* Put your finished list in a safe, easy-to-find place. You'll need it later.

Daily Rewards

Let's begin by looking at some options for the daily rewards you could use.

• **Free time.**   Most children like to be able to earn short periods of free time, when they can choose something they want to do. Younger children, ages two to seven, can earn something fun to do with Mom or Dad, such as reading a story, playing a game, going on a short walk, going for a bike ride, coloring, playing with toys, watching cartoons, or anything else that's easy and fun. Older children, ages eight to twelve, may choose to spend their free time watching television, listening to music, playing games (including video games), talking on the telephone, goofing around, or whatever else they enjoy. Which of these fun-to-do, free-time activities would be good rewards for your child? Can you think of other easy-to-do, readily available activities she would like to do in her free time?

• **Having a food treat.**   Some families use food treats as a reward and others don't. The Behavior Game will work with or without using food as a reward. When food is used as a reward a child usually can earn one or two food treats each day. Children may get a food treat after school or after dinner or before bed.

• **Being with friends.**   Regardless of their age, most children like to do things with friends. A short, one-to-two-hour visit with a friend is usually a good reward. Does your child like to have friends over or go to a friend's house?

• **Bedtime rewards.** For younger children, a good bedtime reward is being read an extra story. If your child is young, would she like an extra fifteen-minute story before she goes to bed? For older children a good bedtime reward is staying up thirty minutes later than usual. Even though staying up later delays bedtime by thirty minutes, most parents find this is such a powerful reward that they're willing to let their child stay up the extra time.

• **Earning money or colorful stickers.** Money can be a very effective reward, particularly with older children. They can earn small amounts of money by performing good behaviors, perhaps five or ten cents for each good behavior. Many parents encourage their children to save up their money and buy things they want. Some younger children like earning small amounts of money as well. Other younger children aren't interested in money or buying things but do enjoy earning colorful stickers for being good. Do you think your child would like earning five or ten cents or a colorful sticker for good behavior?

• **Other daily rewards.** What other daily rewards do you think your child would like? Be sure to include these on your checklist.

Weekly Rewards

Although weekly rewards tend to be bigger than daily rewards, they should still be easy to give and readily accessible. When picking weekly rewards remember that it's best to give them during the weekend when there's more time and opportunity to do things. Here are some ideas:

• **Weekend activities.** This reward can include doing something and/or going somewhere during the weekend with a friend or with the family. Your child might want to go to a movie, out to lunch, or to the mall. She may want to rent a video to watch with a friend. She may want to have a friend spend the night, or she may want to go to a friend's house. Do you want to include this category as a weekly reward? Where do you think your child would like to go? What would your child like to do?

• **Getting something new.** Children love to get "stuff." Most children can come up with inexpensive things they'd like to have, perhaps an inexpensive toy, book, art equipment, hair ribbons, sports cards, or a music tape. Older children may actually buy these things with their money rewards, while younger children can pick something out as a weekly reward. What kinds of "little" things would your child like? Do you want to include "getting something new" as a weekly reward?

• **Other weekly rewards.**   Can you think of other weekly rewards your child might like? Be sure to include these on your checklist.

You don't have to use all the daily or weekly rewards I just mentioned. Some families don't use food; others don't use money. Use only those rewards (and in those amounts) that make you comfortable.

Monthly Rewards

Sometimes older children want to save up for a bigger reward, perhaps a special compact disk or video game. If your child wants to be able to save up for rewards, you can include a category of monthly rewards. Your child may also want to save up and earn enough check marks to do something special like going to a sports game or a play or a music concert. This kind of activity can also be a monthly reward.

As you're putting your finishing touches on your Reward Checklist, let's check in with the Bradleys as they complete Cindy's and Bobby's lists. (See sample lists on the following pages.)

As Gary and Joan reviewed the list of rewards you just read about, they decided that Cindy and Bobby would especially like free time, staying up later, and earning money.

Both children loved free time. Cindy always had a million things she wanted to do, such as paint or color. Bobby loved playing video games.

And both children would probably do almost anything for the chance to stay up later. Cindy always found an excuse not to go to bed on time. It seemed as though she'd beg her parents every night to let her stay up just a little longer. Usually they let her because arguing with her was so unpleasant. Without question, staying up later would be a powerful reward for Cindy and Bobby as well. Joan and Gary also decided to offer earning money as a reward so that Cindy and Bobby could buy little things or save up for something special.

Joan and Gary were pretty sure that Cindy and Bobby would like all of the weekly rewards on the list, especially going out for lunch, shopping, or

Reward Checklist

For _Cindy Bradley_

Instructions: Check each reward that you want to include in your child's Behavior Game. *Any of these would be fine. Checked those we think Cindy would like best.*

DAILY REWARDS
15 minutes of free time
- ☐ Be with Mom or Dad
- ☐ Read a story
- ☐ Play a game
- ☐ Go for a walk
- ☐ Play with toys
- ☑ Watch television
- ☑ Listen to music
- ☑ Talk on telephone

Other fun things
- ☐ _____
- ☐ _____
- ☐ _____

Food treat
- ☑ _Fruit-flavored candy_
- ☐ _____

Being with friends
- ☑ Have a friend over (_Ellen_)
- ☑ Visit a friend
- ☐ Other_____

Bedtime rewards
- ☐ Extra bedtime story
- ☑ Stay up 30 minutes later
- ☐ Other_____

Earning money
- ☑ For good behaviors

Other rewards
- ☐ _____
- ☐ _____

WEEKLY REWARDS
Weekend activities
- ☑ With Mom or _Dad_
- ☑ With friends (_Ellen_)
- ☑ See a movie
- ☑ Go out to lunch
- ☑ Have a friend overnight
- ☑ Go to a friend's house

Other fun things
- ☐ _____
- ☐ _____
- ☐ _____

Getting something new
- ☑ An affordable toy/game/_book_
- ☐ Rent a game or video
- ☐ Sports item
- ☑ Clothes, stuff to wear

Other new stuff to get
- ☑ _Paints_
- ☑ _Hair ribbons_
- ☐ _____

MONTHLY REWARDS
Not sure yet
Saving up for
- ☐ _____
- ☐ _____

Other rewards
- ☐ _____
- ☐ _____

Reward Checklist

For _Bobby Bradley_

Instructions: Check each reward that you want to include in your child's Behavior Game. *Any of these would be fine. Checked those we think Bobby would like best.*

DAILY REWARDS
15 minutes of free time
- ☑ Be with Mom or Dad
- ☐ Read a story
- ☑ Play a game
- ☐ Go for a walk
- ☑ Play with toys
- ☑ Watch television
- ☐ Listen to music
- ☐ Talk on telephone

Other fun things
- ☐ _____
- ☐ _____
- ☐ _____

Food treat
- ☑ _Fruit-flavored candy_
- ☐ _____

Being with friends
- ☑ Have a friend over
- ☑ Visit a friend
- ☐ Other _____

Bedtime rewards
- ☑ Extra bedtime story *or*
- ☑ Stay up 30 minutes later
- ☐ Other _____

Earning money
- ☐ For good behaviors

Other rewards
- ☐ _____
- ☐ _____

WEEKLY REWARDS
Weekend activities
- ☑ With _Mom_ or Dad
- ☑ With friends
- ☑ See a movie
- ☑ Go out to lunch
- ☑ Have a friend overnight
- ☑ Go to a friend's house

Other fun things
- ☐ _____
- ☐ _____
- ☐ _____

Getting something new
- ☑ An affordable _toy/game_/book
- ☑ Rent a game or video
- ☑ Sports item
- ☐ Clothes, stuff to wear

Other new stuff to get
- ☐ _____
- ☐ _____
- ☐ _____

MONTHLY REWARDS
Not sure yet
Saving up for
- ☐ _____
- ☐ _____

Other rewards
- ☐ _____
- ☐ _____

to a movie. Cindy also liked pretty clothing, such as hair bows and socks. Bobby loved to rent video games and get small toys. All of these were inexpensive and would be good weekly rewards.

After you've finished filling out your Reward Checklist it's a good idea to put it in the same easy-to-find place that you put your completed Good Behavior Checklist. You'll be referring to these lists when you make up your child's Game.

Do Kids Really Want These Rewards?

Over and over again, my clients ask, "How can such everyday things be rewards? Will my children actually work to earn little stuff like free time?" When I first started teaching parents to play the Behavior Game, I remember wondering the same thing myself. But my clients assured me that when the Game was used correctly, easily available, small rewards always worked. Let's see what happened when my client Peter Sawyer introduced the idea of small rewards to his son, Scott.

When I first discussed using inexpensive rewards with my client Peter, he was skeptical because his nine-year-old son Scott seemed interested only in costly toys or sporting equipment. Every Sunday morning at breakfast, as Scott looked through the paper, he'd rattle off a list of all the things he couldn't live without—a new pair of skates, a championship baseball bat, a remote-control car. He had to have all of them, he'd tell his dad. Understandably, Peter was concerned that Scott wouldn't consider activities such as free time or staying up later as rewards. Fortunately, Peter's fears were unfounded. Although Scott didn't give up his dreams of getting big rewards, as he played the Game he eagerly worked to earn smaller daily rewards.

As I think back, I realize that even my own children amazed me with how much they wanted to earn little rewards such as free time or going to the store to get a treat. When they were young, I'd buy them a little treat on the way home from work. When I got home we'd look over their charts, and if they'd had a good day they'd get the treat. Day after day, they were excited to get this treat as a reward. When they got older, staying up later became their favorite reward. They'd do almost anything for the privilege of staying up later.

I recommend that all of my clients, parents and children alike, have a list of rewards to pick from. So continue your reward selection by coming up with some rewards that you like.

INCLUDING REWARDS JUST FOR YOU

The Game works best if everybody, including you, has rewards to look forward to. To make this easy for you, I've constructed a *Parent* Reward Checklist, which contains rewards my clients have enjoyed. Before making up your own list, let's take a look at the lists Joan and Gary Bradley made up.

Parent Reward Checklist

For _Joan Bradley_

Instructions: The following list contains rewards that my clients have enjoyed. Check off those things and activities you'd like to include as your own rewards. Add any others as well.

Most sound great! I checked what I like best.

DAILY REWARDS
- ☑ Take a walk, get some exercise
- ☑ Watch television, write a letter, talk to a friend, listen to music
- ☑ <u>Read a book</u>, look at the newspaper, flip through a magazine
- ☐ Fool around with your computer, learn about something new *Too much like work*
- ☐ Cook, sew, or garden
- ☐ Work on the car or a home-improvement project
- ☑ Just do nothing for a few moments
- ☑ Other *Spend time by myself where it's quiet*

WEEKLY REWARDS
- ☑ Try to get away for a few hours, go somewhere, and do something
- ☑ Go out for dinner, see a movie, go shopping *All of these!*
- ☑ Play a sport, <u>go on a long walk</u>
- ☑ Just do something fun or do nothing at all
- ☐ Other _____

Parent Reward Checklist

For *Gary Bradley*

Instructions: The following list contains rewards that my clients have enjoyed. Check off those things and activities you'd like to include as your own rewards. Add any others as well.

Rewards for parents. What a great idea.

DAILY REWARDS

☑ Take a walk, get some <u>exercise</u>

☑ <u>Watch television</u>, write a letter, talk to a friend, listen to music

☑ Read a book, <u>look at the newspaper</u>, flip through a magazine

☑ Fool around with your computer, learn about something new

☐ Cook, sew, or garden

☑ Work on the car or a home-improvement project *Sometimes fun*

☐ Just do nothing for a few moments

☑ Other

WEEKLY REWARDS

☑ Try to get away at least for a few hours, go somewhere, and do something

☑ Go out for dinner, see a movie, go shopping *All of these!*

☑ <u>Play a sport</u>, go on a long walk *Shoot hoops at the park*

☑ Just do something fun or do nothing at all

☑ Other *Go to a sporting event*

Now that you've seen what Joan and Gary chose, please take a few moments and fill out your very own reward list.

To Do

1. *Copy:* Make a copy of the Parent Reward Checklist for yourself and spouse if he/she is playing. You'll find this list in Appendix A.
2. *Fill out:* Check off the rewards you'd like to have and add any others.
3. *Save:* Put your completed list in a safe, easy-to-find place. Let it remind you to reward yourself.

After you've made up your reward list, do at least one of the fun things you wrote down as soon as possible. But no matter what, try to give yourself a small reward at least once a day. Getting rewards for all your efforts will help you stay motivated to keep playing the Game.

Congratulations! You know the foundations of the Game. It's time to begin chapter 2 and learn how to translate these fundamentals into two single-page charts to use with your child when he plays the Game.

2

MAKING UP YOUR CHILD'S BEHAVIOR GAME CHARTS

In this chapter you'll learn how to complete a special two-page chart I developed to help you and your child play the Behavior Game. The first page is called the Good Behavior Chart. It lists all the kinds of good behavior you want your child to exhibit and provides spaces where you can put stars or check marks when this good behavior occurs. The second page is the Reward Chart. It allows you to make up a reward system you can use on a daily, weekly, and, if needed, monthly basis. You and your child will refer to these charts frequently. And, as I'll explain in chapter 3, you'll keep using these charts for as long as you play the Game. Each week when you begin the Game, you'll use a fresh Good Behavior Chart for your child, and if you've made any changes in your child's rewards you'll make up a fresh Reward Chart as well.

My clients find that using a written chart helps on a number of fronts. It provides a record of improvement that your whole family can see. The chart reminds you to reward good behavior. It encourages your child to be good so he can earn stars or check marks. In fact, most children are so proud of their charts that they want them posted on the refrigerator or in some prominent place so that everyone can see how well they're doing.

Now it's time to begin filling out the Good Behavior Chart. (See sample on the following page.)

COMPLETING THE GOOD
BEHAVIOR CHART

By filling out a Good Behavior Chart for your child, you are determining the good behavior you want to see and then deciding how many stars or check

Good Behavior Chart

For _____ / From _____ To _____

GOOD BEHAVIOR	SUN.	MON.	TUES.	WED.	THURS.	FRI.	SAT.
Getting up on time (___)							
Getting dressed							
Taking care of self							
Eating breakfast nicely							
Being ready for school (___)							
Other							
Getting along with • Brother/sister (___min.)							
• Friends (___min.)							
• Parents (___min.)							
Doing what is asked							
Doing chores							
•							
•							
Doing schoolwork (___min.)							
•							
•							
Eating dinner nicely							
Other							
Getting ready for bed (___)							
Going to bed (___)							
Staying in bed							
Other							
Daily Total							

Weekly Total		

marks your child will earn for each of these kinds of good behavior. Take as much time as you need with this critical Game preparation. Be aware, however, that you will be revising this chart as experience with the Game dictates and your child's behavior improves.

To help you come up with definitions for the kinds of good behavior you're going to include on your child's chart, follow the guidelines below:

• **Make your definitions as specific as you can.**   The Behavior Game works best if you have a very precise definition of exactly what your child must do in order to accomplish each kind of good behavior and earn a reward, check mark, or star. At this point you may find it helpful to refresh your memory by reviewing the Good Behavior Checklist in chapter 1.

• **Define each kind of good behavior so that your child can achieve it fairly easily.**   Make sure your child is able to do what you put on his chart. If the behavior is too difficult and your child can't do it, he'll lose interest in the Game. You may want to refer to the ratings you made on your child's Good Behavior Checklist to help you decide what you can expect of your child and for how long. As you remember, on this checklist you rated how frequently your child displayed good behavior, whether he did so often, sometimes, rarely, or never.

• **For behavior that rarely happens, it's a good idea to start with low standards for what you consider "good."**   For example, if your child rarely cleans her room, make it as easy as possible for her to earn a star for cleaning her room by requiring only that she put away her dirty clothes or that she put away her toys. If your children rarely play nicely together, use short times for getting along, such as five or ten minutes. If your child hates to do schoolwork and rarely does it, reward doing homework for short amounts of time and focus on the subject areas she does best. As you read through the descriptions below, let your ratings help you decide what standards you want to use for each example of good behavior.

• **Plan to help your child with any good behavior that he finds difficult.**   Don't expect your child to display many kinds of good behavior completely on his own. You'll be encouraging him to do well by reminding him and, when needed, by helping him. Younger children are especially likely to need their parents' help.

• **Be brief and write only limited, important information on your child's Good Behavior Chart.**   It's not a good idea to write down every detail of what you want your child to do. Instead include only the most important information—for instance, times when things have to happen, such as getting up and going to bed. You should also include how long your children need to behave well—for instance, getting along or doing schoolwork—to earn a check mark or star. And you may want to write in brief reminder notes beside each kind of good behavior your child has difficulty remembering. For example, in my family I wrote in reminders for my children to brush their teeth and to put their homework and lunches in their backpacks. I also included eating three bites of each food at mealtime. For chores, I wrote in short descriptions of what they needed to do, such as feeding the cat, putting dirty clothes in the hamper, and helping out when asked. For schoolwork, in addition to each fifteen minutes of studying, I included bringing schoolwork home, knowing when the homework assignments needed to be finished, and being aware of when tests were planned. Let's see how my clients the Randolphs incorporated these ideas.

Although Mimi and Stuart Randolph wanted to put every detail on their nine-year-old daughter Elizabeth's Good Behavior Chart, as we talked about it, they realized there simply wasn't enough room. So they decided to compromise and include written reminders about only those behaviors that Elizabeth was likely to forget. Even though her mom took her lunch out of the refrigerator and put it on the kitchen counter every morning, somehow Elizabeth's lunch bag never ended up in her backpack. When making up Elizabeth's chart, her parents jotted down, "put your lunch in your backpack" in the "other" category in the first section covering morning behavior. Since Elizabeth was developing what her mother considered unacceptable back talk, she included "no smart-mouth talk" next to "getting along with parents." Elizabeth would know what that meant. And since bedtime often involved a grueling interchange over what Elizabeth needed to do to get ready for bed, her dad made sure to squeeze in everything that needed to happen at bedtime on his daughter's chart. Over the first few weeks these notes helped bring Elizabeth's chart to life and made it much easier for her to remember to do the things that were hardest for her.

- **Consider including simple pictures of good behavior for a young child.** If you have a preschool child, words alone may not be very effective. In addition to listing each kind of good behavior, you may want to make a drawing or paste on a picture of it. These pictures can help remind your child of what is expected as well as how he can earn stickers and other rewards. Let's see how my client Mirna Gonzales used this idea when she made up her three-year-old son Juan's Good Behavior Chart.

As Mirna was quick to point out to me, since words didn't have much impact on her son, she had flipped through some old magazines, cut out a number of pictures of what she wanted her son to do, and pasted them on his chart. I was quite impressed with the chart she had made. It included a picture of a toothbrush, a bar of soap, boy's clothing, a bed and a clock, children playing together, and a spoon and fork. Beside each picture there was plenty of room for stars and stickers. Juan was quite pleased with his chart as well. When he showed it to me, he smiled as he pointed to each picture and explained what it meant. After only a few days Mirna was pleasantly surprised because these pictures were already helping Juan learn what he was supposed to do.

To Do

1. *Copy:* For each child who is playing the Game, make a copy of the Good Behavior Chart, which you'll find in Appendix A.
2. *Fill out:* As you fill out a Good Behavior Chart for each child, follow the steps below.
3. *Save:* Put your finished chart in a safe, easy-to-find place. You'll need it soon.

Step 1. Specify Each Good Behavior You'd Like to See

As you fill out the Good Behavior Chart, consider how you want to define each kind of behavior and what brief notes you want to include on your child's chart:

• **Getting up.** When is wake-up time going to be? Most families choose an early wake-up time so that everyone isn't too rushed. Don't expect your child to get up completely on his own; plan on reminding him.

• **Getting dressed.** What behavior do you want to include? Do you plan to remind your child that she needs to get dressed? Do you need to help her pick out clothes? Do you need to help her get dressed? Younger children often need some help getting dressed. Do you need to set a time limit? If your child takes forever to get dressed, a time limit can be helpful.

• **Taking care of self.**   What behavior do you plan to include? Most parents include brushing teeth, combing hair, washing face, going to the bathroom, and washing hands. Do you need to set a time limit? If you use time limits, make certain that they are long enough so that your child can get all of the needed behavior accomplished without being rushed. Do you need to help your child with any of these kinds of behavior? If your child is young, you should plan on helping him with whatever is needed.

• **Eating breakfast.**   What behavior does eating breakfast nicely include? Most parents specify how much they want their child to eat and how they want her to act at the breakfast table. Most parents also use a reminder before breakfast to let their child know what they expect. For slow eaters, parents often set a time limit.

• **Being ready for school on time.**   What behavior does being ready for school on time include? Should your child have his backpack ready with his homework and his lunch? Should he be wearing a jacket? What else does he need to do? You may want to give advance notice five minutes before it's time to be ready for school so that your child has time to get everything ready and thus can accomplish what you expect of him.

• **Getting along.**   How do you want to define getting along? Most parents include sharing, helping each other, cooperating, and playing together without fighting, yelling, or name-calling. You may want to include a brief reminder about any difficult-to-remember behavior such as no teasing or name-calling.

How long do you want your children to get along in order to earn a star or check mark? Most parents choose relatively short amounts of time for their children to get along, from five to fifteen minutes. As you continue playing the Game and your children are getting along better, you can increase the time periods required for getting along. But at the beginning, it's best to choose short periods for getting along. However, even if you are lucky enough to have children who can get along right now, you should consider rewarding them three times per day for getting along in the morning, the afternoon, and the evening. *No matter how well your children get along, never require your children to get along for the entire day in order to earn a check mark or star.*

• **Doing what is asked.**   How do you want to define this kind of behavior? To most parents it means responding to a request the first time it is made without a hassle or argument, within a short amount of time. The request can be about anything, so long as it's reasonable. It may be asking a child to help out with a younger brother, to turn down the television, to listen, or to do something "now."

• **Doing chores.** What chores do you want your child to do? Most families require that their children do at least one chore every day. Chores can lighten the parents' workload, but of equal importance, they help teach children responsibility.

When you start using the Good Behavior Chart don't overload your child with chores. At most, include only three easy ones that you and your child can do together or that your child already knows how to do. One chore may be as much as your child can handle for now. The following list contains suggestions of chores from which you can pick: cleaning his room, helping Mom or Dad straighten up, helping at mealtime, helping with laundry, or taking care of a pet.

Cleaning one's room. You might initially define this chore as putting the dirty clothes in the hamper or in a dirty clothes pile and picking up and putting away toys. In a week or two, after your child has mastered these two tasks, you might add straightening up the bed and putting away clean clothes.

Helping Mom or Dad straighten up around the house. This chore could include putting trash in the wastebasket, putting away toys, and taking dirty dishes to the kitchen. Again, after your children have mastered these, you could add dusting or vacuuming or whatever else you need help with.

Helping at mealtime. You can use these same ideas when coming up with tasks your children can help you with at mealtime. Do you want them to help you set the table, cook, clear the table, do the dishes, or take out the trash? Again, make sure the tasks you choose are fairly easy ones that they can already do.

Helping with the laundry. If you'd like your child to help you with the laundry, how would you like her to help you? Do you want her to bring her dirty clothes to the washing machine, help load the washing machine, help unload the dryer, help fold clean clothes, and/or put them away?

Taking care of pets. In some families children have been promising to take care of their pet(s) since well before the pets arrived. The Behavior Game is an excellent time to get your child to do this. If you want your child to take care of his cat or dog or other pet, define the tasks you'd like to see happen: feeding the pet, cleaning up after the pet, and/or walking the pet.

Whatever chores you choose, you might consider doing them with your child for the first several days to make sure she knows what you want her to do. It's also important to help her when she needs it and to use plenty of praise and encouragement. With chores, like any other kind of good behavior, you shouldn't expect perfection.

•   **Doing schoolwork.**   As part of their Good Behavior Charts, most families include at least some examples of school-related behavior that require concentrating and paying attention to a task. The school-related behavior you choose will depend on the age of your child and what he is required to do. Your child's teacher may be able to help you decide on what behavior is the best to include, but here are some suggestions, broken down by grades:

For preschoolers and kindergartners.   You can give a child in this age range tasks that will help her learn skills she will need for school, such as concentrating, paying attention, and completing tasks. Some examples are coloring, putting together a puzzle, or doing blocks. You will probably need to perform the task with her initially so she is comfortable and can ask you questions about it. Make these tasks easy and the amounts of time devoted to them short. Most of the parents I work with pick between two and four tasks for their child to perform. Tasks tend to take between five and fifteen minutes each. Spread them out over the afternoon and evening.

For first through third graders.   If you have a child this age he is probably beginning to have some homework. The Behavior Game can help him learn to bring his work home from school, do it at home, and take it back to school.

At this age I recommend you choose short amounts of time, perhaps five to fifteen minutes, for doing schoolwork. You may want to reward your child not just for completing her work, but also for accomplishing each step involved in the process of getting her work done. You can also reward your child for trying to do the work and checking it over. Don't punish your child if she makes mistakes. Remember that perfection is not the criteria for good behavior and rewards.

Some children have a great deal of difficulty doing schoolwork; others do not. The behavior you choose for your child's chart will depend on what your child is capable of and willing to do. Some kinds of behavior you can choose include: bringing schoolwork home, knowing what work needs to be done, doing five to fifteen minutes of schoolwork, trying to do schoolwork and concentrating on it, and remembering to take schoolwork back to school.

For fourth through seventh graders. Homework usually becomes harder and more time consuming as your child moves from fourth to seventh grade. You can use the Game to encourage your children in these grades to develop responsibility, to bring their homework home, to do their work at home, and to take it back to school. It can also help you avoid constantly nagging your child to do homework and threatening consequences if it is not done.

You should reward your child for completing each part of her homework, not just for finishing it. I recommend study periods lasting about 15 minutes. You can also encourage your child to do extra work or to work ahead, especially to study ahead of time for tests.

Some kinds of schoolwork behavior you can choose are bringing homework home; studying for fifteen minutes; completing homework in each subject; letting you know about upcoming assignments, tests, and reports; working on schoolwork ahead of time; doing extra schoolwork of any kind; and taking homework back to school.

Future parts of this book cover school problems in more detail and suggest ways to work effectively with your child's teacher.

• **Eating dinner nicely.** What kind of behavior do you want to see at dinner? Most families include coming to dinner when called, sitting at the table until dinner is over, using silverware, and talking in a pleasant, civil manner. Some families also include no name-calling, no food throwing, no spitting, no poking, and no chewing with mouth open. My clients differ considerably when it comes to how much food they expect their child to eat. Although I don't recommend that you require your child to clean her plate, I do think it's a good idea to ask her to eat at least three bites of each food. If you have a slow eater you may want to add a time limit as well.

You may find that it helps your child if you give him advance notice that dinner will be ready in five or ten minutes. This will enable him to finish whatever he's doing and prepare for dinner. A reminder at the beginning of dinner about what is expected is also helpful.

• **Getting ready for bed.** What behavior do you want to see at bedtime? Parents usually include brushing teeth, washing face, going to the bathroom, putting on pajamas, and when needed, taking a bath and washing hair.

There may be other behavior you want to include, depending on how well your child does all these things. Your child may need help with some or all of these kinds of behavior, especially if she's younger. Think about how much time you need to allow for this process, what time it should start, and how long it should last.

As with dinner, it may help if you give advance notice five or ten minutes before it's time to start getting ready for bed, and then, when it's time to begin getting ready, give a reminder about what has to be done.

• **Going to bed on time.** What time do you want to make bedtime? What do you want your child to do when he goes to bed on time? Most parents want their child in bed and lying down with his head on the pillow when it's bedtime. And, they want their child to remain lying down as they say good night and leave the room. If your child is earning staying up later as a reward, then you'll need to give him this extra time on the days he earns this reward.

• **Staying in bed.** It's a bit tricky to define what staying in bed means. It's obviously a good idea to allow your child to get up when it's truly necessary, such as when she needs to use the bathroom or if she is ill. But children can be very creative about why they have to get up. Try to stand your ground, but be flexible at the same time.

• **Other kinds of good behaviors.** Write in any other kinds of good behavior you want to include and define them briefly if needed.

Step 2. Indicate How Many Stars or Check Marks Each Kind of Good Behavior Will Earn

Most kinds of good behavior on your child's Good Behavior Chart should earn one check mark, star, or sticker. Each time your child performs one of the kinds of good behavior listed on the chart, you should put a check mark, star, or sticker on his chart. Whether you use check marks, stars, or stickers will depend on which one is easiest for you and which your child likes best. Older children, eight and above, often prefer check marks, while children five to seven like getting stars and stickers. If your child is a preschooler, you probably won't have to make any hard-and-fast rules about how many stars or stickers each kind of good behavior will earn.

Let's look at an example of how earning one star for each kind of good behavior would work for your child in the morning when it's time to get up and get ready for school. If your child gets up on time, he can earn a star; if he gets dressed without a hassle, he can earn a star; if he takes care of himself and brushes his teeth, washes his face, and combs his hair, he can earn a star; if he eats breakfast nicely he can earn a star; and finally, if he's ready to leave for school on time he can earn a star. If your child has a good morning and performs all of the kinds of good behavior listed on the morning section of his chart, he can earn five stars.

If your child has particular difficulty with certain kinds of good behavior, you may want to offer more than one star or check mark for doing these things. For example, if your child is having trouble getting up in the morning or going to bed on time at night you may want to let her earn two stars for accomplishing either task. If it's especially hard for her to do her schoolwork or get along with her brother or sister, you can consider giving her more than one star or check mark for these kinds of behavior.

I've found that it's better to err on the side of giving more rather than fewer stars or check marks for good behavior, especially at the beginning of the Game. On your child's chart make a note beside any kinds of behavior that will earn more than one check mark or star. Let's see how my clients, Louise and Frank Washington, used an added check mark to encourage their son, Dennis, to do his school assignments.

Would ten-year-old Dennis ever finish his homework without a major struggle erupting between him and his parents? Begging, reasoning, pleading, threatening no more television or video games—Louise and Frank had tried them all but nothing worked. Dennis was developing into a professional procrastinator when it came to his schoolwork. So when they were assigning check-mark values, Louise and Frank decided that he could earn two stars for every ten minutes spent on homework. Dennis liked this idea from the moment he first heard about it. Gradually, his schoolwork improved. Looking forward to extra stars seemed to help him sit down, concentrate, and do his assignments.

In my family it was obvious from the very beginning that "going to bed" and "staying in bed" would both qualify for extra stars. My children hated doing both of these. I knew I was willing to do almost anything to make this nightly ordeal more bearable.

And finally, before you finish your Good Behavior Chart, let's look at sample charts for Cindy and Bobby and then see how the Bradleys decided which behaviors should earn extra check marks.

Good Behavior Chart

For _Cindy Bradley / first week_

GOOD BEHAVIOR	SUN.	MON.	TUES.	WED.	THURS.	FRI.	SAT.
Getting up on time (7 A.M.)							
Getting dressed							
Taking care of self _Teeth, hair, face_							
Eating breakfast nicely							
Being ready for school (7:45)							
Other							
Getting along with • Brother/sister (5 min.)							
• Friends (15 min.)							
• Parents (15 min.) (2✓ w/Mom)							
Doing what is asked (2✓)							
Doing chores _Feed Freckles_							
• _Clean room_							
• _Help w/dinner_							
Doing schoolwork (15 min.)							
• _Work alone or with parent_							
• _Bring home / take back schoolwork_							
Eating dinner nicely							
Other							
Getting ready for bed (7:30)							
Going to bed (8:30)							
Staying in bed							
Other							
Daily Total							

Weekly Total	

Good Behavior Chart

For _Bobby Bradley / first week_

GOOD BEHAVIOR	SUN.	MON.	TUES.	WED.	THURS.	FRI.	SAT.
Getting up on time (7 A.M.)							
Getting dressed (2✓)							
Taking care of self _Teeth, hair_ (2✓)							
Eating breakfast nicely							
Being ready for school (7:45)							
Other							
Getting along with • Brother/sister (5 min.)							
• Friends (15 min.)							
• Parents (15 min.)							
Doing what is asked							
Doing chores							
• Clean room							
• Help w/dinner							
Doing schoolwork (10 min.)							
• Go over work with Mom or Dad							
• Read with Mom or Dad							
Eating dinner nicely							
Other							
Getting ready for bed (7:00)							
Going to bed (8:00)							
Staying in bed							
Other							
Daily Total							

Weekly Total

In the Bradley family, since Cindy was rarely ever civil to her mother, her parents decided she should earn two check marks for getting along with her mother and for doing what was asked. Bobby had so much trouble getting going in the morning that they decided to give him two stars for getting dressed without a hassle and for brushing his teeth and combing his hair.

Once you have decided how many stars or check marks your child can earn by performing each kind of good behavior, you've finished the Good Behavior Chart and it's time to move on to the Reward Chart.

COMPLETING THE REWARD CHART

The second page of your child's Behavior Game chart is the Reward Chart. As you fill out this chart you'll indicate the following things: which daily, weekly, and, if needed, monthly rewards you want your child to be able to buy; how much each one costs; how many times per day, week, or month each one can be bought; and when your child can cash in and spend her stars or check marks to buy rewards. (See sample on the next page.)

Your child will refer to the Reward Chart when deciding how to spend the stars and check marks he's earning. As you did with the Good Behavior Chart, plan to spend a day or two completing this chart.

No matter how old your child is, the following sections on daily, weekly, and monthly rewards should prove helpful as you make up your child's Reward Chart. However, if you have a two-, three-, or four-year-old, before making up a chart for her be sure to read through the special section for young children at the end of this chapter. It will give you ideas on how to tailor your reward system to meet the specific needs of your preschool child.

To Do

1. *Copy:* For each child who is playing the Game, make a copy of the Reward Chart, which you'll find in Appendix A.
2. *Fill out:* As you fill out a Reward Chart for each child, follow the steps below.
3. *Save:* Put your finished Reward Chart in a safe, easy-to-find place. You'll need it soon.

Reward Chart

For _____ / From _____ To _____

DAILY REWARDS		
15 minutes free time	Cost	x/Day
Be with Mom/Dad	____	____
Read a story	____	____
Play a game	____	____
Go for walk	____	____
Play with toys	____	____
Watch television	____	____
Listen to music	____	____
Talk on phone	____	____
Other_____	____	____
_____	____	____
Food treat	____	____
_____	____	____
Being with friends		
Have friend over	____	____
Visit a friend	____	____
Other _____	____	____
Bedtime rewards		
Extra story	____	____
Stay up 30 min. extra	____	____
Other _____	____	____
Other rewards	____	____
_____	____	____

Getting money

Each star/check mark = ____

Maximum earned each day = ____

Daily Cash-in Times	
After school	Before bed
Before dinner	As needed

WEEKLY REWARDS		
Weekend activities	Cost	x/Wk
With Mom/Dad	____	____
With friends	____	____
See a movie	____	____
Rent movie/game	____	____
Go to lunch	____	____
Have friend overnight	____	____
Visit friend	____	____
Other _____	____	____
_____	____	____
_____	____	____
_____	____	____
Getting something new and affordable		
Game, toy, book	____	____
Sports item	____	____
Clothes	____	____
Other _____	____	____
_____	____	____
_____	____	____
_____	____	____

Weekly Cash-in Times
During weekend as needed

MONTHLY REWARDS		
Saving up for	Cost	x/Mon
_____	____	____
_____	____	____
_____	____	____
_____	____	____
_____	____	____

Step 1. Make Up Your Daily Reward System

As you read through the rewards described below you'll notice that they tend to be inexpensive, usually costing from one to five stars per day. By using low prices, you'll guarantee that your child can "buy" at least two or three rewards each day. So long as your child is getting rewards, he should stay motivated to play the Game. You'll also find a suggestion to curb the number of times your child can buy any particular reward. It's usually a good idea to set a limit of one to four times per day that a specific reward can be bought. This restriction encourages your child to buy different rewards throughout the day and helps keep the Game from getting boring. It also prevents him from being able to buy the same reward repeatedly, such as watching television or playing video games.

Keeping these general considerations in mind, let's look specifically at each daily reward you may have chosen, what it should cost, and how often you should allow your child to buy it.

• **Free time.**   Offer a variety of free times. Use time periods of fifteen minutes. Have each fifteen-minute period cost five check marks. Allow each type of free time to be bought up to four times per day.

• **Food treat.**   Have each food treat cost five check marks or stars. Allow food treats to be bought two times per day.

• **Being with friends.**   Have playing with friends for one to two hours cost ten stars or check marks. Allow your child to visit with friends at most once per day. If you feel that every day is too often for your child to get together with friends, consider letting your child see friends two or three times per week. And, of course, before you set up this reward, be sure to check with friends' parents for their okay.

• **Bedtime reward.**   If you have younger children, offer an extra bedtime story. Have it cost five stars and make it available only once per day at bedtime. If you have an older child, offer her the chance to stay up thirty minutes later than her usual bedtime. Have this reward cost ten check marks and make it available only once per day.

• **Earning money or stickers.**   If you included earning money as a reward, you need to decide how much money each star or check mark is worth. When doing this, choose an amount you're comfortable with. If your child is young, consider making each star worth five cents; if your child is older, eight and above, consider making each check mark worth ten cents. When deciding how much money your child can earn each day, think about letting a younger child earn up to $1.00 per day and an older child $1.50 per day. For children under five, consider using colorful stickers instead of money.

• **Other daily rewards.**   List any other rewards you want to use, how much they will cost, and how often per day your child can buy them.

Step 2. Set Up Daily Cash-in Times

Cash-in times are specific times during the day when your child can turn in her stars or check marks to buy daily rewards from her Reward Chart. Regardless of age, all children need at least two cash-in times per day when they can spend their stars or check marks to buy rewards. For younger children more frequent cash-in times work best.

Make up a plan with both fixed and flexible cash-in times. Many families have a system in which they offer two fixed cash-in times: one after school or when Mom or Dad gets home from work, and one thirty minutes before bedtime. They often include additional cash-in opportunities as needed throughout the day and evening, depending on how many stars and check marks their children are earning. If your child is doing well and getting his schoolwork done, getting his chores accomplished, and getting along with siblings, offering him a chance to buy rewards can provide a welcome break and give him an opportunity to enjoy a little free time before going back to work.

At the end of the day, after your child has gotten ready for bed, but at least thirty minutes before bedtime, you can set up her last cash-in time. At this point your child can spend any stars or check marks she has left from the day on a reward such as staying up thirty minutes later or reading an extra story with Mom or Dad. If she has any check marks left after buying this reward, she can turn them in for money.

Since it's difficult to reward going to bed and staying in bed when these are happening, most parents award the stars or check marks earned for these behaviors the next morning and give their children the opportunity to spend these stars or check marks the next day. For example, if your child goes to bed on time and stays in bed on Sunday night, he would get to spend the stars he earned on Monday.

Each family comes up with its own plan for cash-in times. Some children want to save up most of their stars or check marks and convert them into money. Other children may want to save up to be sure they have enough stars or check marks to buy the reward of staying up thirty minutes later. On the other hand, some children may want to buy a reward as soon as they have enough stars or check marks.

As long as your child has enough stars or check marks to buy a reward, it's okay for her to request a cash-in time. If it's a convenient time, let her cash in and buy a reward. If it's not a convenient time, let your child know when she will be able to cash in. For example, you may be in the middle of fixing dinner when your child wants to buy the reward of playing a game with you. When this happens, suggest some other rewards that can be bought and/or promise that you'll play a game as soon as you can. Of course, be sure to follow through and play the game with your child.

As a general rule, most families with younger children find it best to end the day with a zero balance of stars or check marks. They encourage their children to spend all the stars or check marks they've earned. When you try to carry stars over to the next day, young children often get confused because the concept is too complicated for them to understand.

To make daily cash-ins go smoothly, keep a record of how many stars or check marks your child spends during the day. You can mark off what she spends by putting a diagonal line through each star or check mark that your child uses to buy a reward. Or you can color in each box after the star or check mark has been spent. Keeping this kind of record helps everyone know what has been spent and what hasn't and eliminates arguments about how many stars or check marks are still available to spend.

Step 3. Make Up Your Weekly Reward System

On the Reward Chart you'll find a list of weekly rewards. Keep those you want to use and add any others. After that you can assign a price to each one and specify if there's a limit to how often your child can buy them. When deciding on how much each weekly reward should cost and how often each one should be bought, keep these recommendations in mind:

Have each weekly reward cost twenty-five stars or check marks. With this system, if your child is earning between five and ten check marks per day, he'll be able to buy at least one and probably more weekly rewards.

Allow each weekly reward to be bought only once per weekend. This will encourage your child to buy different weekly rewards.

Allow your child to buy up to three weekly rewards each week. Usually three weekly rewards is enough. If she has stars or check marks left over she can save them for a bigger monthly reward.

Step 4. Set Up Weekly Cash-in Times

At the end of the week your child should have the opportunity to cash in all of the stars or check marks he earned during the week to buy his weekly rewards. Although he has already spent his stars or check marks every day, he gets to spend them again for weekly rewards.

In the Behavior Game, I strongly recommend that you allow your child to spend his stars or check marks once for daily rewards and then again at the end of the week for weekly rewards. Most of my clients find that when stars or check marks have this double value the Game works best, because children are motivated by immediate daily as well as more long-term weekly rewards. If your child has extra check marks remaining after buying her weekly rewards, she can save them for monthly rewards.

And, although you may be talking throughout the week with your child about what he wants to do on the weekend to spend his check marks, it's a good idea to try to have a meeting every Friday afternoon (or whenever else works for you) to add up his check marks and decide when, during the weekend, he can cash them in to buy his weekly rewards. Come up with a schedule that's convenient for everyone involved.

Your family's schedule for weekly cash-in times may vary from week to week depending on which rewards your child wants to buy and what other activities are going on. For this reason, it's a good idea to plan on having flexible rather than fixed cash-in times during the weekend.

Let's see how the Bradleys used these suggestions to make up a daily and weekly reward system for their children Cindy and Bobby, and then take a look at the charts they developed.

Joan Bradley's teaching schedule fit well with Cindy and Bobby's timetable. Every afternoon, after everyone got home and had a chance to touch base about their respective days, Cindy and Bobby would count up their check marks from the morning and cash them in for an afternoon reward. Bobby almost always retired to his room for thirty minutes of video games. Since his parents were worried that if given the chance that would be all he ever did, they limited his video time to one hour per day. Cindy, on the other hand, could care less about "those silly cartoon games" as she called them. She liked to spend her free time playing with Ellen, her best friend who lived next door. To keep Cindy from overdoing this reward, she was limited to visiting with Ellen three afternoons during the week. At night both children always chose one of their most treasured rewards, staying up later and watching television for thirty minutes. If they had any remaining check marks at the end of the day, they converted them into money. On the weekends, in between soccer games, Cindy chose going to Ellen's house or had her over as a weekly reward. She also liked to go shopping with her mom or dad and get art supplies or what she called "fashion accessories" such as hair ribbons, pins, and assorted jewelry. Bobby also liked doing things with friends and shopping but chose action toys or sports cards instead of that "stupid girl stuff." By splitting up and each taking one child shopping for his or her weekly reward, Joan and Gary were able to spend some positive one-on-one time with each of their children. (See their sample charts on the following pages.)

Step 5. If Needed, Make Up a Monthly Reward System and Set Up Cash-in Times

If you and your child have picked some monthly rewards, you should list these on her chart, and then, depending on how big the monthly reward is, assign a price of fifty, seventy-five, or one hundred stars or check marks for each reward. It's a good idea to allow your child to buy only one or two monthly rewards per month.

As noted above, when buying monthly rewards your child can use only those extra check marks not already spent on weekly rewards. For example, if your child earns one hundred twenty-five check marks in a week, he could spend seventy-five on weekly rewards and save the remaining fifty check marks for a monthly reward.

Once she has earned enough check marks for a monthly reward, discuss what she wants to buy or do and come up with a convenient time for this to happen.

After you've decided on your child's monthly reward system, you should be finished filling out his Reward Chart.

Reward Chart

For *Cindy Bradley / first week*

DAILY REWARDS

15 minutes free time — Cost / x/Day
- Be with Mom/Dad ___ ___
- Read a story ___ ___
- Play a game ___ ___
- Go for walk ___ ___
- Play with toys ___ ___
- Watch television — 5 — 2
- Listen to music — 5 — 2
- Talk on phone — 5 — 2
- Other ___ ___ ___
- ___ ___ ___

Food treat *Candy* — 5 — 2
___ ___ ___

Being with friends
- Have friend over *or* — 10 — 3x wk
- Visit a friend ___ ___
- Other ___ ___ ___

Bedtime rewards
- Extra story ___ ___
- Stay up 30 min. extra — 10 — 1x day
- Other ___ ___ ___

Other rewards ___ ___
___ ___ ___

Getting money
- Each star/check mark = *5 cents*
- Maximum earned each day *20✓ ($1.00)*

Daily Cash-in Times
After school	Before bed
Before dinner	As needed

WEEKLY REWARDS

Weekend activities — Cost / x/Wk
- With Mom/Dad — 25 — 1
- With friends — 25 — 1
- See a movie — 25 — 1
- Rent movie/game ___ ___
- Go to lunch — 25 — 1
- Have friend overnight — 25 — 1
- Visit friend — 25 — 1
- Other ___ ___ ___
- ___ ___ ___
- ___ ___ ___

Getting something new and affordable
- Game, toy, book — 25 — 1
- Sports item ___ ___
- Clothes — 25 — 1
- Other *Paints* — 25 — 1
- *Hair ribbons* — 25 — 1
- ___ ___ ___
- ___ ___ ___

Weekly Cash-in Times
During weekend as needed

MONTHLY REWARDS

Play these by ear; let Cindy buy when she can afford.

Saving up for — Cost / x/Mon
- *Special clothes* — Varies — 1
- *Special event* — Varies — 1
- ___ ___ ___
- ___ ___ ___
- ___ ___ ___

Reward Chart

For _Bobby Bradley / first week_

DAILY REWARDS

15 minutes free time

	Cost	x/Day
Be with Mom/Dad	5	2
Read a story	5	2
Play a game	5	2
Go for walk	5	2
Play with toys		
Watch television	5	2
Listen to music		
Talk on phone		
Other_____		
_____		

Food treat _Candy_	5	2
_____		

Being with friends

Have friend over _or_	10	2x wk
Visit a friend		
Other _____		

Bedtime rewards

Extra story _or_	5	2x day
Stay up 30 min. extra	10	1x day
Other _____		

Other rewards

_____		

Getting money

Each star/check mark = _5 cents_
Maximum earned each day _10✓ ($.50)_

Daily Cash-in Times

After school	Before bed
Before dinner	As needed

WEEKLY REWARDS

Weekend activities

	Cost	x/Wk
With Mom/Dad	25	1
With friends	25	1
See a movie	25	1
Rent movie/game	25	1
Go to lunch	25	1
Have friend overnight	25	1
Visit friend	25	1
Other _____		
_____		
_____		

Getting something new and affordable

Game, toy, book	25	1
Sports item _Small_	25	1
Clothes	25	1
Other _____		
_____		
_____		
_____		

Weekly Cash-in Times
During weekend as needed

MONTHLY REWARDS

Play these by ear; let Bobby buy when he can afford.

Saving up for

	Cost	x/Mon
Sports items	_Varies_	1
Special event	_Varies_	1
_____		
_____		
_____		

The following section applies specifically to making up a reward system to use with preschool children. If your child is five or older, you may want to skip this section and move on to the next chapter about how to incorporate the Game into your family's daily life.

Step 6. If Needed, Make Up a Special Reward System for Young Children

If you're playing the Game with a child who is two, three, or four years old, you'll probably find that she doesn't need a formal Reward Chart in which each reward is worth a specific number of stars. Instead, her Reward Chart can simply list daily and weekly rewards without any indication of how many stars need to be earned in order to get rewards. You may want to include a simple picture of each reward as well.

To decide on the rewards you want to use, it's a good idea to review the Reward Checklist you have already made up. You probably checked some of the following rewards, which work well with children this age: Doing something fun with Mom or Dad, playing with toys, watching cartoons, playing a game, going for a walk, playing with friends, reading a story, coloring, and getting a sticker or a small treat.

Throughout the day you can decide when you want to give these rewards and you can choose which rewards to give, or you can show your child her list and let her pick which reward she wants. Most children in this age group are quite happy with this informal, rather "spur of the moment" type of system in which you decide when and what the rewards are. Let's take a look at the way my client Anna used this informal type of reward system with her three-year-old daughter Carol.

In addition to getting a lot of stickers on her chart, Anna made sure that her daughter got to do some fun activities. Carol was a rambunctious child who seemed to be constantly in motion, so going to the park and playing on the swings was a favorite activity. Fortunately the park was just down the block, so this trip was an easy reward for Anna to give Carol. Usually at midmorning Anna would go over all the stickers on Carol's chart and review why she'd gotten them, whether it was for getting going in the morning, playing nicely, or minding her mom. Then she'd let Carol know that it was time for a reward and suggest that they go to the park before lunch. In the afternoon after

Carol's nap, her mom often took her on a walk with their dog as a reward. On days when it was raining, Anna would play a game or watch a video with her daughter as a reward. As a special reward, sometimes her dad Ralph brought home ice cream or a cupcake for Carol to have for dessert. Carol seemed very happy with this combination of stickers, doing things with her mom, and special dessert treats. Anna and Ralph were pleased not only with how quickly this system helped Carol improve but also with how much Carol liked getting rewards and doing things with them.

Be sure to give your preschooler at least three rewards each day. A young child needs to get rewards as immediately as possible. He doesn't do well if he has to wait for a reward or settle for a promise that a reward is coming later. I recommend that you use a system in which you immediately put a sticker or star on his chart for each good behavior, and then as soon as you can, offer him a reward such as a little treat or a fun activity.

Every evening do a daily review of how your child did and how many stars she earned. Many clients I work with have told me how delighted and proud their children are each night as they look at all their stars or stickers and count them up. This is a good time to give your child praise, encouragement, and hugs for her efforts and to give her a reward for all her hard work, perhaps extra story time or a game with Mom or Dad.

Be sure your child knows what he's being rewarded for. When you present a daily reward make certain to link up the good behavior your child has displayed with the reward he's earning. When you make this connection, your child will begin learning that good things happen when he behaves well. To help him learn this, always tell your child what he did to earn a reward as you give it to him.

When you've finished your preschooler's Reward Chart, it's time to turn to the next chapter to find out how to make giving rewards part of your daily schedule.

3

MAKING THE GAME PART
OF YOUR FAMILY'S LIFE

Making the Behavior Game work involves much more than just putting your child's chart up on the refrigerator and giving check marks or stars when he or she is well behaved. The Behavior Game must become a basic part of your life rather than simply a piece of paper you look at from time to time. So before you put the Game into action, it's a good idea to consider carefully these tips on how to make the Game a central part of your daily life:

• **Maintain a calm, optimistic attitude.** The way you approach the Game makes a big difference. If you can be calm, positive, and patient, you will be much more successful than if you are hurried, demanding, and impatient. Being calm, positive, and patient also helps create an atmosphere of trying, cooperating, and sharing. Throughout the day, give yourself an attitude check to see how you're doing. If you're tense or irritable, try to relax for a minute, take a deep breath, and regroup.

Many parents have told me that if they had known how their children would react to the Game, they could have been more calm, more consistent, and more positive. Unfortunately, there's no way to predict exactly what your child will do. However, by thinking ahead about how you'll approach the Game and getting yourself in the right frame of mind, it will be much easier to be at your best.

• **Encourage the whole family to work together as a team.** The Behavior Game should not be a battle between parents and children. In fact, when played correctly, the Game creates a "win-win" situation—parents get the kind of good behavior they want and children earn the rewards they want.

• **Talk about the Game with enthusiasm.** Throughout the day go over your child's Game and let him know how he's doing, the positive ways he's behaved, and the stars or check marks he's earned. You can also preview the Game for him by highlighting what's coming up later in the day or the next morning, and what he can do to earn more stars or check marks.

• **Give frequent advance notices, reminders, and assistance.** Help your children learn what you want them to do and how the Game works by frequently giving them calm and pleasant advance notices and reminders. This will help them remember what they're supposed to do and the rewards they're going to earn. When they need help being well behaved make sure you're there to assist them.

• **Praise your child frequently.** Especially at the beginning, the more you tell your child how well she's doing the better she will do. Throughout the day make sure to recognize your child's success by giving her praise and encouragement and by giving her stars or check marks for good behaviors. If you don't naturally tend to give verbal rewards, make an extra effort to change and become more positive and demonstrative.

• **Be yourself, of course, but however you do it, also be rewarding.** If you use humor continue to do so. If you're very critical try to save the criticism and not mix it with praise. Especially when you start the Game, try to limit your criticism and never criticize a child who's trying.

• **Put stars or check marks on your child's chart when he behaves well.** Don't put this off. Don't forget to do it. If it makes your job easier, have your child remind you to put up stars or check marks. Your children need to see the stars or check marks they have earned.

• **Provide your child with enough opportunities to cash in his stars or check marks to buy rewards.** As you know, for the Game to work your child must earn stars or check marks and be able to spend them to buy rewards. To make sure this happens, you should set up several cash-in times throughout the day when your children can buy rewards with their stars or check marks.

• **Give yourself credit for a job well done.** At least two or three times a day, take a minute to pat yourself on the back for all the time and effort you're putting in.

Now let's take a look at ways you and your family can incorporate the Game into your daily lives from the minute you get up and until the time you go to bed.

PLAYING THE GAME IN THE MORNING

Even if you and your child are not "morning people," the Behavior Game can help the whole family begin the day on a brighter note. What your family has to accomplish in the morning will depend on whether your child needs to get ready to go to school or child care or whether he'll be staying home with a parent or a baby-sitter.

If your child is staying home, your routine can be more relaxed, but she'll still need to get up, get dressed, and eat breakfast. And before you know it, she'll be old enough to be heading off to school. So it can't hurt to start using these tips to get things going in the morning, no matter how young your child is.

• **Make wake-up time early enough that you and your children have time to get ready.**   If you don't have enough time in the morning and you're rushed and frantic, it will be very difficult to use the Behavior Game effectively. Especially when you begin using the Game, you may need to take extra time to make certain that your child behaves well and earns stars or check marks. At least for a while you may need to get up a little earlier to make sure that the Game gets off to a good start.

To help your child get up on time make sure he knows when wake-up time is. Give him advance notice ten minutes before it's time to get up, and then when it's get-up time, return to his room and remind him to get up.

• **Remind your children about what they are expected to do in the morning.**   Be certain that your child knows what you want her to do in the morning. Is she supposed to get up, get dressed, brush her teeth, wash her face, and go to the bathroom without a hassle? Is she supposed to eat breakfast nicely? Is she supposed to get her backpack ready for school? Does she need to do anything else?

• **End the morning on a positive note.**   When it's time to send your child off to school or day care, it's important to be positive and supportive. Before he leaves, remind him that he can spend the stars he's earned after school or when you get home. Even if the morning has gone terribly and your child did poorly earning stars or check marks, don't end the morning with criticism or negativity. Instead, talk about how everyone can work together to make the afternoon better, and how you're sure that with a little effort your child will be able to earn some stars or check marks and buy some rewards. It's very difficult for your child if you're angry with him when he leaves for the day. He's likely to worry about how poorly the morning went at home and may have problems paying attention in school. So, if you can, avoid being angry when you're saying good-bye.

• **Take a break and congratulate yourself for getting through the morning.** After your child has left for school or you're off to work, it's time for your first relaxation break of the day. Take a minute, think over how the morning went. Celebrate any small victories your family had. Then, if necessary, regroup. And finally, when you're ready, focus on what you need to do for the rest of the day, whether at home or at work.

IF YOUR CHILD IS HOME ALL DAY

If your child is not going to school and is staying home, you can offer him a reward after he's gotten up, gotten dressed and eaten breakfast. Perhaps he can watch a cartoon or a favorite video or do something like play a game or color. Letting your child have a reward is a nice way to end this part of the morning.

Throughout the day, make sure to continue using praise and encouragement to help your child get along with you and do what you ask. Also, be sure your child gets to enjoy frequent, small rewards. Since younger children don't need a structured reward list, you can use your judgment about when you want to give your child rewards.

And don't forget to try to take little breaks for yourself during the day. Squeeze them in whenever you can. Perhaps at nap time or when your child is busy with a toy or game, you can sit down for a minute, take a few deep breaths, and try to relax.

IF YOU'RE AT HOME IN THE AFTERNOON WITH YOUR CHILD

Before your child comes home, take some time to prepare yourself. Put yourself in the right mood. Remind yourself about how important it is to let your child know you're glad to see him. Here are some ways to do that:

• **After school, take some time to share the day's experiences.** During this time with your child, listen to what she has to say, have fun, and "hang out." Try to show interest without being judgmental or critical.

Don't cross-examine your child about school, but try to listen with an open mind as she talks about how her day went. And of course, offer support and understanding.

• **Offer your child an after-school cash-in time.**   After your child has had the chance to unwind from school, you can offer a cash-in time so that he can buy a reward with the stars or check marks he earned in the morning. When reward time is over, it's time to get started with schoolwork and chores.

• **Go over what everyone has to do and get each one started.**   Review your child's Behavior Game and go over what schoolwork and chores she needs to do. Remind her that she can also earn stars and check marks for getting along and doing what is asked. Help her decide how she's going to accomplish everything she needs to do. What should she finish before dinner? What should she finish after dinner? If necessary, make up a schedule for the rest of the day. Start your child off by having her work on the first task on her schedule. Check in with her from time to time to see how things are going.

• **When possible, take short breaks and offer cash-in times.**   As your children are doing their work or getting along together, be sure to keep their Games up-to-date by entering stars or check marks as they earn them. You can offer cash-in times throughout the afternoon to allow your child to buy rewards for finishing parts of his homework or his chores, for doing what is asked or getting along with his siblings.

Children usually do best if they can take breaks from homework or chores from time to time. So long as they've earned stars or check marks and want to spend them, you can offer a cash-in time and let your child take a break.

Again, throughout the afternoon, you should take short breathers yourself. Concentrate on the things that are going well and remind yourself that no one's perfect, not your child and not you, either.

IF YOU GET HOME AROUND DINNERTIME

On your way home it's helpful to switch gears from a work mode to a family mode. If you're frustrated about work, remind yourself not to take it out on your family. Try to be upbeat and positive. Prepare yourself to be as calm and supportive as possible. Here are some tips on how to make the most of the time you have before dinner:

• **When you get home, make time for you and your child to share her day's experiences.**   Spend some time with your child even if it's only five minutes. Let your child know how happy you are to see her. Find out how her day went. Try to listen and not ask too many questions. Just "hang out" with her, even if only for a short time.

• **Offer a before-dinner cash-in time.**   After everyone has had a chance to touch base with one another, offer a before-dinner cash-in time when your child can spend some of the stars and check marks he's earned during the day. After reward time is over, if there's still time, have your child begin his home-work or chores as you get dinner ready.

If you're away from your child all day, you may be thinking about having the person who takes care of your child use the Game while you're at work. *It's best to wait until you've used the Game for a week or two yourself before you involve your baby-sitter or day-care provider.* You'll find specific sugges-tions on how to do this in chapter 6. But for now, concentrate on teaching yourself how to use the Game and make it part of your daily life.

PLAYING THE GAME IN THE EVENING

Here are some tips to make your evening as productive and pleasant as possible:

• **Alert your family when it's dinnertime.**   As dinner is starting, get your family in the mood for a nice dinner by reminding everyone about how im-portant having a pleasant dinner is, how you expect everyone to get along during dinner, and how stars and check marks can be earned. If you want help with dinnertime chores, remind your child about what she's supposed to do.

• **During dinner, let your child know when he's doing well.**   Comment throughout the meal about how well things are going and give stars or check marks for good behavior and/or for helping out with dinnertime chores.

• **After dinner, map out everyone's schedule.**   Quickly review your child's Game and have a family discussion about what everyone plans to do. It's also a good idea if parents take this opportunity to share the things they hope to accomplish during the evening. By doing this, your child will learn that he's not the only one who has things that need to get done.

• **Get everyone started, monitor each one's progress, and offer cash-in times when needed.**   Check in with your child frequently to find out how she's doing and how many stars or check marks she's earning. When she has enough stars or check marks, offer a cash-in time. If your child is saving up her stars or check marks to buy a bedtime reward or to turn them in for money, she may not want to spend them during the evening.

PLAYING THE GAME AT BEDTIME

Bedtime is often the hardest time of day for families. Children are tired and can be irritable and difficult to deal with. Parents are likely to be tired, as well, and may find their patience in short supply. Again, using the Game can help the whole family make bedtime a better experience. Here are some tips on how to survive bedtime:

• **Remind your child when it's time to start getting ready for bed.**   Give your child enough time so that he can do all the things he's supposed to in order to get ready for bed. When you're just starting to use the game be sure to remind him about what you want him to do. Does he need to take a bath? Wash his hair? Wash his face? Brush his teeth? Go to the bathroom? Put on his pajamas?

• **After your child is ready for bed, take some more time to talk about your child's experiences for the day.**   Begin by talking about your child's day and what else may have happened. As always, be sure to offer support and understanding. After you're done talking about her day, review her Game with her. As you look over your child's Game, talk about all the good things she did, all the stars and check marks she earned, and all the rewards she bought.

Add up all the stars or check marks he earned during the day and put them in the daily total box. Remind your child that he can spend these stars or check marks again on the weekend for weekly rewards. If your child wants to, talk about what weekly rewards he's hoping to buy. Figure out how many stars or check marks he has left to spend, and then, talk about what rewards he'd like to buy with them before he goes to bed.

• **Offer a final cash-in time when your child can buy a bedtime reward.** For older children this reward is likely to be staying up later; for younger children it's likely to be an extra bedtime story.

If your child has stars or check marks left after buying her bedtime reward, encourage her to turn them in for money. It's usually easiest for everyone if your child spends all her stars before she goes to bed.

- **Give an advance notice about bedtime.** Give your child an advance notice that bedtime is coming, maybe ten to fifteen minutes ahead of time. Remind your child about the stars or check marks he can earn for going to bed on time and staying in bed.
- **Tell your child when it's bedtime and put her to bed.** Be fair but also be firm. Be positive but brief. Say a quick good night. Remind your child that she can earn stars or check marks for going to bed now and staying in bed, and then leave your child's bedroom. Of course, there will be times when you'll need to alter this bedtime routine, such as when your child is sick or unusually upset.

Enter the stars or check marks your child earns for going to bed and staying in bed on his Game. In the morning make sure to show him these stars or check marks and remind him that he can spend them later in the day.

At the end of the day when your child is in bed, pat yourself on the back and congratulate yourself on completing the day. While you're doing this, think over how your day went. What were the things that went well? What didn't work well? What times of day were the easiest? The most difficult? Try to figure out what you can do tomorrow to make the rough times smoother. Perhaps you need to be more positive; perhaps you need to use more advance notices and reminders; or perhaps you need to offer more cash-in times. Resolve to keep trying to be upbeat, calm, and positive. Keep rewarding your children's good behavior, and yours, too! And, if you have the energy, try to take a few minutes for yourself before you collapse and go to bed.

PLAYING THE GAME ON THE WEEKEND

The weekend is a time for your children to cash in their stars and check marks and buy weekly rewards. It is also a time for your family to celebrate the victories of the week and to have fun. *Relaxation* and *fun* are important words here. Your pace can slow down and your family can try to enjoy each other and spend a little free time together.

Over the weekend it's a good idea to use a relaxed version of the Behavior Game. You can still give stars or check marks for behavior that involves getting along, doing what is asked, and generally being nice to family and friends, but you might want to relax requirements for getting up, doing chores, doing schoolwork, and going to bed. Most of the families I work with find that weekend Behavior Games also need to be flexible to accommodate their family's weekend activities.

Weekends should allow each family member, including parents, some time off from chores and tasks, some time to do nothing at all. So try to do less. Try to get some rest so you're energized and ready to start playing the Game again when Sunday afternoon rolls around.

Remember to offer weekly cash-in times over the weekend. You may want to get together on Friday afternoon or evening to count up the daily check marks or stars your child has earned and to decide on weekly rewards. Remember that your child can use all the stars or check marks he earned during the week to buy his weekly rewards. Even if during the week your child spent all of his check marks every day on different activities, he can use them again to buy his weekly rewards. Stars or check marks can be spent twice—once for daily rewards and once for weekly rewards.

It's usually not difficult for your child to decide on the weekly rewards because she's been thinking about them all week long and already knows what she wants. However, be forewarned that sometimes your child will want more than she can afford. It's important that you permit your child to buy only what her stars or check marks will allow. Don't give her advances and don't let her buy rewards she can't afford—she'll have plenty of time to operate like that after she's making her own money and has credit cards!

I hope these tips help you make the Game a major part of your family's life. To make it easier for you to remember these suggestions, I've summarized them on the Parent Daily Checklist, which is included here and in Appendix A. My clients as well as my own family have found this checklist helps take the worry out of what to do next. In fact, many parents rely on the information included in the Parent Daily Checklist so much that they put it up on the refrigerator right next to their children's Game.

To Do

1. *Copy:* Make a copy of the Parent Daily Checklist, which you'll find in Appendix A.
2. *Save:* Put it with your child's chart so it's easy to find when the time comes to put the Game into action.

Parent Daily Checklist

EVERY DAY, THROUGHOUT THE DAY . . .

Adopt a calm, positive attitude.

Talk with your child about the Game.

Give frequent advance notices, reminders, and help.

Praise your child for good behavior.

Put stars or check marks on your child's chart.

Provide enough cash-in times.

Give yourself credit for your efforts.

When possible, enjoy a reward from your list.

IN THE MORNING . . .

Wake up early so your family has time to get ready.

Let your children know what they need to do.

Remind them they can spend their stars after school.

IN THE AFTERNOON . . .

If you're home with your children:

Get in the right frame of mind.

After school, allow time to discuss the day's experiences.

Offer an after-school cash-in time.

Go over what everyone has to do and get each one started.

When possible, take short breaks and offer cash-in times.

If you work and get home around dinnertime:

When you get home, allow time to discuss the day's experiences.

Offer a before-dinner cash-in time (if possible).

If there's time, have your children begin schoolwork.

AT DINNERTIME . . .

Prepare your family for a peaceful dinner.

Let everyone know when each is doing well.

IN THE EVENING . . .

Map out everyone's schedule and get each one started.

Monitor progress and offer cash-in times when needed.

AT BEDTIME . . .

Remind your child when it's time to get ready for bed and what needs to be done.

After your child is ready for bed, take some additional time to discuss the day's experiences.

Offer a final cash-in time when your child can buy a before-bed reward.

Give an advance notice before bedtime.

Make sure your child goes to bed on time.

ONCE YOUR CHILD IS IN BED . . .

Pat yourself on the back.

Review your day and look ahead to tomorrow.

Congratulate yourself—you made it through another day!

ON THE WEEKEND . . .

Play a relaxed version of the Behavior Game.

Be sure your child has a chance to enjoy his or her weekly rewards.

Enjoy your own weekly reward.

Congratulations, you've accomplished a lot. You've gathered the information you'll need to get the Game going and completed the initial important paperwork. You now know more about your kids and what you expect from them. Perhaps you can begin to see the possibility of a saner, happier family life. The work continues, but also the fun begins. Your next step is to put the Game into action.

4

PUTTING THE GAME
INTO ACTION

Here we'll cover everything you need to play the Behavior Game from week to week. To ensure that your child has a positive experience with the Game from the very beginning, I'll provide special tips for introducing the Game and playing on the first day. Then I'll give you some guidelines to help make the first week and weekend go more smoothly, and finally I'll share some suggestions for continuing the Game each week.

INTRODUCING THE GAME

Most of my clients find that Sunday afternoon or evening is a good time to introduce the Behavior Game and then begin playing. If this is a convenient time for your family, plan to spend next Sunday afternoon or evening getting the Game started. If Sunday doesn't work for you, introduce the Game at any convenient time and play for the remainder of the week.

Before you start playing, spend some time talking to your child about the Game. Be sure to emphasize how much fun the Game will be (use the word *game*), and how much everyone will enjoy playing it, including you. And let me assure you once again that kids do enjoy it. When you're talking about the Game, tell your child enough about it so that she understands how it works and what she needs to do to earn check marks or stars and buy rewards. But at the same time, don't overload her with too much information and bore her with an overly detailed explanation. Younger children, especially, are usually eager to get started.

These guidelines should help you walk this fine line between too much and not enough:

• **Be calm and positive.** **Take your time.** Go step-by-step. Don't rush through your explanation. Encourage everyone to listen when you're discussing the Game. If your child gets bored during your explanation or his attention starts to wander, take a short break and then begin again.

• **Go over the reasons your family is going to play the Game.** Let your children know that it will help the family get along better, will help them get their schoolwork and chores done, will help everyone work together, will help Mom and Dad be nicer, and will help the family to be happier. And most important, stress that the game will give them many opportunities every day to earn rewards for their good behavior.

After this general introduction, it's time to go over the Good Behavior Chart you filled out in chapter 2. If more than one child is playing, you may want to review the chart in general for the whole family and then talk individually with each child about her own chart.

• **Review the kinds of good behavior shown on the chart.** Briefly go over each good behavior. Make sure everyone understands what each kind of behavior involves. Let your child know that you'll help her by reminding her of when it's time to do the things you want her to do.

• **Go over how the spaces on the chart work.** Show your child the spaces for stars or check marks. Let your child know that each time he does one of the activities mentioned you will put a star or check mark in the correct space.

• **Review the ways your children can use check marks or stars to buy rewards.** Remind your child that after she has earned check marks or stars for being good she can then use them to buy rewards. Show her the Daily Rewards section of her Reward Chart. Point out that it contains a list of rewards and how much each one costs.

• **Review daily cash-in times.** Let your child know that there will be cash-in times throughout the day when he can spend his stars or check marks to buy rewards. Go over when these cash-in times will happen.

• **Double-check that your child understands the basics you just explained.** If she's old enough, have her explain the Game back to you. If she's young, have her show you where the stars go and ask her to tell you about some of the good behavior you want her to demonstrate. Have her tell you about the rewards she's looking forward to earning. Reassure your child that during the next week you'll be reviewing the chart and how it works at least two or three times a day. Encourage her to ask questions.

Since most children are eager to get started at this point, it's a good idea to wait until later in the week to talk about weekly rewards and the weekend version of the Game.

If your family is hesitant about playing, do your best to talk them into giving the Game a try. Almost all children want to play the Game. If your child isn't sure she wants to play, try to convince her to see what it's like for the next few days and then decide about playing. Most of the children I work with are willing to give the Game a try. Give your child at least two weeks to try it out. In future chapters we'll take a look at some things you can do if your child refuses to play.

If your child starts asking so many questions that you're getting nowhere in your explanation or if she's arguing with everything you say, stop and let her know that you'll continue when she's ready to listen. Let her ask questions when you're finished.

It's not unusual for children to ask for more, whether it's more stars, check marks, or rewards. If this happens to you, be firm. You are in charge of the Game, and it's up to you to decide on its limits. As a rule, stand your ground and don't give in to your children's demands for more.

GETTING IT STARTED

Once you've explained the Game to your child, it's time to put it into action. The following guidelines should help you get off to the right start:

• **Give your child a check mark or star as a reward for listening to your explanation.**   Let him know how pleased you are that he listened when you were talking and put a star or check mark in the "Doing what is asked" box under Sunday.

• **Ask your child if she wants to have her Game displayed so that everyone can see it.**   If she does, have your child help you put up her two-page Game (the Good Behavior Chart and the Reward Chart). Most children, especially younger ones, like to have their Good Behavior Chart in an easy-to-find place, like the refrigerator door, so that everyone can look at it. However, if your child doesn't want her charts displayed that's fine, too. Together, decide on a convenient place where she wants you to keep them, such as in a kitchen drawer or in her room. (From now on, when I talk about your child's chart, I'm referring to her Good Behavior Chart, the first page of the Game.)

• **During the afternoon and evening, set up situations that encourage good behavior.**   Plan one or two fun activities that the whole family can do together and put stars or check marks on the chart when everyone is getting along. Pick activities that your family likes, such as taking a walk or playing a game together.

• **You can also choose several easy chores that are on the chart and encourage everyone to help you complete them.**   In addition, you can have your child do any unfinished schoolwork. Make sure that your child earns check marks or stars for helping with these chores and doing schoolwork.

• **As soon as your child has earned enough stars or check marks to buy a reward, offer a cash-in time.**   Give your child a chance to buy her first reward as soon as she can afford it. It's okay if your child doesn't want to cash in her check marks right away but wants to save them up for a bigger reward, such as staying up 30 minutes later.

• **During dinner make sure that good behavior earns stars or check marks.**   Dinnertime is a good opportunity for the family to talk about what's happened during the day, what's going to happen during the evening, and what family members have planned for tomorrow. Participating in this kind of family discussion should earn a star or check mark.

• **During the evening, continue encouraging good behavior.**   Check in with your child and see how he's doing. If he's earned enough stars or check marks and wants to buy a reward, offer him a chance to cash in.

• **Have your child get ready for bed on time.**   Go over what you want her to do and help her out as needed. After she's ready for bed, review her chart with her and let her know what a good job she did. Add up the stars or check marks she's earned and put the total on her chart. Preview how the Game will work tomorrow and for the rest of the week.

• **Offer a before-bed cash-in time if your child has enough stars or check marks to buy a reward.**   If your child has enough stars or check marks, let him spend them on an extra story or staying up 30 minutes later. If he has any remaining stars or check marks after buying this reward, encourage him to exchange them for money.

• **At bedtime, put your child to bed.**   Remind her that she can earn stars and check marks for going to bed on time and for staying in bed.

• **Pat yourself on the back.**   After your child has gone to bed, pat yourself on the back. You did it! You got the chart started. You made it through the first day. Take a breather and reward yourself.

PLAYING THE GAME FOR THE FIRST WEEK

The first week can be a rocky one, as your family adjusts to the Game. It helps to prepare yourself to begin each day on a positive note. Every morning get yourself in the right frame of mind before beginning the Game. Remind yourself that you're just getting started and that everything won't go perfectly. Your child will make mistakes and so will you. But if you give it a chance, everyone will get the hang of the Game.

Also, refer often to your Parent Daily Checklist. Let it remind you of what you need to do and when you need to do it. If you haven't already done so, you may want to put this checklist up next to your child's Game so that it's easy for you to find.

As you go through the first week, concentrate on helping your child become comfortable with her chart and rewards. And if you're tempted, don't make any hasty changes. Allow your child some time to adjust to this new system.

No matter how fantastic a job you're doing, there will be problems and surprises when you begin playing the Game. So as the need arises, return to this list of ways to handle common start-up problems:

• **Don't force the Game on family members who don't want to play.** If one of your children refuses to play, let him watch as his brothers and sisters earn stars and buy rewards. You'll be surprised at how quickly he changes his mind. If your spouse doesn't have time to get involved in the Game right now or is hesitant about using rewards, that's okay. Give your spouse a chance to watch what happens. As your child starts earning rewards and behaving better, everyone usually warms up to the Game. Encourage your child to share all the good things that are happening with other family members.

• **Don't put bad marks on the chart.** The chart is for good marks only— stars, check marks, or stickers. If good behavior doesn't occur, don't put a bad mark on the chart. Instead, leave the appropriate box blank. The consequence for *not* doing the good behavior is *not* getting a star or check mark.

• **Don't take away stars or check marks after they've been earned.** Even if you're furious with your child, don't take her stars or check marks off her chart. Once earned, they should remain on the chart. If you're so angry with your child that you don't want her to spend her stars or check marks at cash-in time, you can make her wait until you've calmed down. Perhaps she'll be allowed to spend her stars or check marks at her next cash-in time, or if you're really angry, perhaps the next day.

- **Never give your child unearned stars or check marks.**   If your child is having a bad day and not earning stars or check marks, resist the temptation to give him a few rewards even though he hasn't earned them. Don't get caught in the trap of thinking you'll give him an unearned star "just this once." Your child must *earn* the check marks or stars you put on his chart.
- **Make the Game a little easier if your child can't earn at least five stars per day.**   Your child needs to earn rewards to stay motivated. So if after a few days he can't earn enough stars to buy a reward, lighten up a little by lowering your standards or adding some "easy-to-do" activities. You may want to shorten the times required for getting along or doing homework. You can also offer your child assistance for any chores that are giving her difficulty. The important thing is that your child be successful and earn rewards. So if you need to make the Game easier, do it. In chapter 6 you'll learn some tips for raising your standards and requiring more responsibility.
- **Try ignoring problem behavior.**   Whenever possible, try ignoring your child's irritating behavior that gets on your nerves. For more serious problem behavior do whatever you normally would so long as you don't use physical punishment or threats of physical punishment. In chapter 5 you'll learn a variety of discipline techniques to use with your child's problem behavior.
- **Do not use physical force with your child, no matter what.**   No matter how badly your child behaves, don't use physical force or punishment as a means of trying to stop the problem. In chapter 5 you'll learn more about why there is no place for this type of punishment in the Behavior Game.
- **Expect your children to complain about each other's charts.**   Especially at the beginning, brothers and sisters often protest about how unfair each other's charts are. An older brother is likely to complain that his younger sister's chart is so easy she can earn stars for doing nothing. A younger sister may protest that her older brother gets better rewards than she does.

If this happens, briefly explain to your children why their charts are different from one another and then stand your ground. As you remember, charts can vary for a number of reasons, such as the age of the child and the particular problems you want to work on. You may want to highlight the special advantages of each of your children's charts and leave it at that. Be sure your children understand that you don't intend to change their charts. Usually, once children get involved in their own charts and are earning stars or check marks, they stop protesting so much. They may, however, continue to complain some about their brother's or sister's chart. Do your best to ignore this complaining.

•   **Wait to work on any problems your child has away from home.**   After the Game has made things better at home, you can begin using it for behavior that happens outside of the home, at school, or when you're visiting or shopping. In later chapters you'll look at how to use the Behavior Game to help with out-of-home problem behavior.

•   **Remember that it takes time to get used to the Game and there's no teacher better than experience.**   There is no substitute for being in the trenches and actually playing the Game. The first few days may be rough as your child tests the limits of the Game to see if you really mean it. By giving rewards only when your child earns them, you'll be sending your message loud and clear. You do mean it. The Game is in full force. There's no turning back now.

•   **If you have a two-parent household, try to find time to talk with each other every day about how the Game went.**   You may want to set up a time after your children have gone to bed when you can share the day's highlights and disappointments. You can also talk about how you plan to tackle tomorrow's activities. When needed, boost each other's morale and always acknowledge the hard work that others are doing.

•   **If you head a one-parent household, consider finding a "buddy" to talk to about the Game when you feel the need.**   Try to find a supportive, interested person who is in agreement with what you're doing. It almost always helps to be able to run things by another person and get some feedback.

•   **When you want recognition for your efforts, ask for it, if necessary.** Even though it may feel funny, let your family and friends know how hard you're working and how much their encouragement and praise mean to you. Help them get in the habit of telling you what a great job you're doing.

•   **Don't throw in the towel.**   After a tough day, you may find yourself wondering why you're trying so hard and getting so little in return. No matter how discouraged you get, don't give up. Try to take it one day at a time.

It's a good idea not to dwell on the problems your family may have using the chart. Think of every day as a new opportunity for your family to get along better. If yesterday was awful, try to forget it and start fresh. If yesterday was great, build on that success. Expect ups and downs. Some days will go well; others won't. The important thing is to not give up. Keep playing the Game. Over time, things will get better.

Let's see how my clients the Bradleys coped with these common start-up problems:

When Joan Bradley returned home from her evening class the look on her husband Gary's face was unmistakable, he had not had a good evening. Joan soon found out why. It seemed like Cindy and Bobby couldn't do anything right. No sooner had he come home than they started complaining about each other's charts. Bobby insisted that Cindy had earned too many check marks for doing her schoolwork during the afternoon; while Cindy couldn't stop talking about how easy Bobby's chart was. At dinner, they seemed to be competing for who could be the most obnoxious. And after dinner, all they did was argue and fight. Neither had earned any check marks since Gary got home. This was a radical departure from the last few days when Cindy and Bobby had done very well, each earning enough check marks to buy several rewards. What was wrong? Had the Game quit working after only a few short days? Perhaps Gary's co-worker was right on the money when he told Gary that a bribe system like the Behavior Game couldn't work over time because it was artificial and manipulative.

After listening patiently, Joan urged Gary to calm down and try to forget about his evening. She offered to put the children to bed and recommended that Gary find something relaxing to watch on television. After a night's sleep, Gary felt much better—reenergized and ready to continue with the Behavior Game no matter what his friends at work thought about it.

Gary was right to be optimistic. As soon as Cindy and Bobby got up, they started earning check marks for being good and getting ready. In fact, they were all fired up about how to spend their check marks when they got home that afternoon. Instead of dwelling on how bad yesterday had been, Gary and Joan agreed to focus on today and make the most of it.

When we met again, I congratulated Joan and Gary for putting this "bad day" in the past and not rehashing it with Cindy and Bobby. I shared with them that in my clinical experience when parents talk endlessly about what goes wrong and why, they usually slow down the progress they're making with the Game and decrease their children's motivation to change.

PLAYING THE GAME ON THE WEEKEND

At the end of the first week, preferably on Friday afternoon or evening, talk with your child about his weekly rewards and his weekend Behavior Game.

Even though you may already have touched on the weekend Game during the week, it's a good idea to spend some time talking about it again. Explain how the weekend Game will work. Let your child know that during the weekend you expect him to continue getting along, doing what is asked, doing weekend chores, and generally being nice to family and friends, but that requirements for behavior such as getting up, doing schoolwork, and going to bed will be relaxed.

Now is also a good time to talk with your child about how she gets to respend the stars or check marks she earned during the week. Remember, that even though your child spent her stars or check marks every day for daily rewards, she also gets to spend them again to buy weekly rewards.

Together, go over your child's weekly rewards and decide which ones he can buy over the weekend. If your child is not familiar with this list, spend some extra time talking about how much each reward costs and how often each week he can purchase it. If you have a limit on how many weekly rewards your child can buy each, let him know that as well. If you plan to include monthly rewards you can also talk about how these will work.

After you and your child have figured out which rewards she can afford to buy during the weekend, come up with a schedule for when she can enjoy these rewards. Try to pick times that are convenient for the family.

Many children look forward to going shopping with their parents for their reward. If you plan a shopping outing, be sure to remind your children about the kind of reward you'll be looking for, give them specific examples, and set a maximum price that the reward can cost. If your child is earning stickers, the weekend can be a good time for him to pick out stickers for the coming week. Whatever the purpose of your outing, try to enjoy being with your children and take your time. If your child takes forever picking out just the right reward, set a time limit and let him know when he has five minutes left to make up his mind about what he wants.

Start your weekend Game on Friday evening after you've introduced it. Keep it as relaxed as possible. If your family tends to be busy over the weekend, plan on being as flexible as possible when it comes to the Game. Encourage everyone to have a little fun and enjoyment. You and your family have earned some time off and the right to do less and lay back a little. Remind yourself that it's okay to do nothing and to just hang out for a while. Make sure your child gets to enjoy the weekly rewards she's earned. Now's a good time to reenergize yourself, take a break before you begin the Game again, and consider some rewards you'd like to earn.

Once you've made it through the first week, you'll be using the suggestions below to help you play the Game from week to week.

KEEPING THE GAME GOING
FROM WEEK TO WEEK

Before you renew the Game each week, take a moment to make sure that the Game hasn't gotten too hard or too easy. Sometimes parents and children get carried away and the Game becomes too demanding and complicated, and becomes a source of stress rather than pleasant and rewarding. If you're requiring too much of your child or if he's requiring too much of himself, you need to step back a bit. If your child never has a free moment or seems upset and frantic about earning stars, the Game is probably putting too much pressure on him.

As you know, it's very important that your child enjoy the Game and succeed by earning stars or check marks and buying rewards. If she feels like a failure because she can't earn rewards, the Game needs to be changed. So when in doubt don't overdo it, and cut back if necessary. Let's see how my clients Rodney and Diana Evans used these suggestions to help their daughter Sheila:

Hoping to earn a "million" check marks and buy everything she'd always wanted, ten-year-old Sheila Evans talked her parents into an elaborate Game, one that they considered too demanding. However, because their daughter was so adamant they reluctantly agreed to give it a try. What sounded manageable to Sheila in the abstract was anything but when she started trying to do everything on her chart. She'd insisted on including cleaning her room, doing the laundry, feeding and walking the dog, cleaning the hamster cage, helping with dinner, cleaning up after dinner, doing all her schoolwork, reading for thirty minutes per day, and practicing the piano thirty minutes per day. After several days it became clear to everyone that there simply wasn't time for Sheila to do everything. She needed to cut back. Her parents helped her realize that her expectations were unrealistic, that no one could do all the things she'd included. Together they revised her chart by deleting doing the laundry, reducing the amount of help she needed to provide at dinnertime, limiting practicing the piano to only ten minutes a day and making extra reading optional since Sheila already had a fair amount of homework. These changes made it possible for Sheila to accomplish everything and have some time to enjoy her earned rewards.

On the other hand, if your child has lost interest, you may need to tighten up a bit. If your child doesn't think the Game is worth his time and effort because he's already getting plenty of rewards for doing nothing, there won't be much reason for him to stay involved in the Game. For example, if your child is allowed to watch television whenever he wants, he may not bother making the effort to clean his room or study so that he can buy watching television as a reward. If this is happening in your family, change the Game so that your child needs to earn most of his rewards instead of getting them for "free." Let's see how my clients the Monroes used this idea with their son Jamie.

After several weeks, Jane and Dick Monroe realized their eight-year-old son Jamie was losing interest in the Game. As they reviewed a typical day, they concluded that Jamie got to do pretty much what he wanted. After school his baby-sitter let him watch television or go out and play for as long as he liked. When they got home from work, they always spent time playing with Jamie. After dinner he never failed to change the subject when they asked about homework, and at bedtime he was full of excuses about why he needed to stay up later. It wasn't until his report card came that Jamie's parents recognized that things had to change. Jamie would have to do his homework and earn the reward of watching television. The days of "free" TV were over.

For some parents, especially working parents who don't get to see as much of their child as they like, it can be hard to knuckle down and require their children to do schoolwork or chores. But in the long run no matter how tired you are or how much of a fuss your child puts up, setting limits and sticking to them is the best policy. So even when your child puts up resistance, don't abandon the Game, and make sure at least some rewards have to be earned.

Keeping those general suggestions in mind, let's take a look at how to get the Game going each week. My clients find the Behavior Game works best if they are consistent about getting it started at the beginning of each week. By following the eight steps listed below, you'll make sure to do everything you need to each week:

To Do—Each Week

1. *Copy:* Make a fresh copy of the Good Behavior Chart for each child who is playing, and if you're making any changes in your child's rewards, make a fresh copy of the Reward Chart. You'll find these forms in Appendix A.
2. *Review:* Each Sunday afternoon or whenever is best for you, get together with your child, review your child's chart from the past week, and highlight your child's continued progress and improvement.
3. *Fill out:* Complete a new Good Behavior Chart and, if needed, a new Reward Chart.
4. *Preview:* Go over how the Game will work for the coming week, paying special attention to any changes.
5. *Post the new chart:* Put the new Good Behavior Chart up on the refrigerator or in a convenient place. If you've changed the Reward Chart replace that as well.
6. *Get started:* Begin playing the Game again.
7. *Refer to the Parent Daily Checklist:* Throughout the week use this checklist as a reminder of what you need to do. It's a good idea to put it up on the refrigerator next to your child's chart. If you haven't made a copy yet you'll find this checklist in Appendix A.
8. *Relax the Game on the weekend:* On the weekend enjoy your weekly rewards and try to have fun together as a family.

Continue to play the Game for a few weeks until it becomes part of your daily routine and you can see solid progress. If, say, after three weeks you feel you've established a foundation for good behavior, then go on to chapter 5 and tackle any special behavior problems your child may have. Don't be concerned, however, if you need more than three weeks before you're comfortable moving on to discipline techniques. Each family progresses at its own pace.

PART TWO

BUILDING ON YOUR SUCCESS

Controlling Problem Behavior,
Raising Expectations, and
Improving Communication

5

GETTING PROBLEM BEHAVIOR UNDER CONTROL

So far you've concentrated primarily on increasing your child's good be-havior. Now, you'll turn your attention to decreasing, even eliminating, problem behavior, the things your child does that really drive you crazy. *But please don't begin this chapter until you've worked through the first four.* Although you may want to jump right in and tackle problem behavior head on, avoid the temptation. Over the years my clients have had greater success when they put their Behavior Game into action and rewarded their child's good behavior first. Then after a few weeks, when their child's behavior had improved, they focused on discipline techniques and how to use them with problem behavior. I recommend that you follow this sequence because it's much easier to get problem behavior under control after your child is earning rewards and is motivated to behave better.

DISCIPLINE TECHNIQUES

There are a variety of discipline techniques that I recommend my clients use to decrease their children's problem behavior. You may already be familiar with some of them. In fact, you may have already tried some of them. If you have, you probably found that some of the time they worked and some of the time they didn't. Fortunately, when you use them along with the Behavior Game, they're likely to work all of the time.

Before you make any decisions about how you want to handle your child's problem behavior, it's a good idea to spend whatever time you need to under-stand all of the discipline techniques described here.

89

Rewarding the Opposite of a Problem Behavior

When you play the Behavior Game with your child and reward good behavior, you are rewarding the opposite of a problem behavior. Sometimes just doing this is enough to decrease or even get rid of a problem behavior.

Why? Because when children are getting rewards for behaving the way you think they should, they're less likely to behave in ways you don't want. Rewarding good behavior, such as getting up on time, may be enough to help your child break the habit of getting up late. Providing a reward for getting dressed without a hassle may encourage you child to get dressed quickly instead of taking forever. Giving stars or check marks for brushing his teeth, washing his face, and combing his hair may help your child remember to do these things instead of forgetting about them. Your child's table manners and appetite may improve dramatically once he's getting a check mark for eating nicely. He may even be able to find his backpack, fill it, and be ready to go to school because he's getting a star on his chart.

Rewarding your child for getting along may help her stop fighting and arguing so much with her brothers, sisters, friends, and parents. Giving stars for doing what is asked may help your child disobey less frequently. Providing encouragement for doing schoolwork may motivate your child to pay attention and finish her homework instead of finding excuses for why she can't do it. Motivating your child to do her chores by offering a star or check mark may help her finish what she starts.

Providing rewards for getting ready for bed and going to bed can often go a long way toward helping your child stop giving you a hard time every night when you try to get him to go to bed.

Not getting their stars or check marks can motivate children to change their behavior. As you know, the only way your child can earn check marks is by performing the activities on her Good Behavior Chart. When she doesn't behave well, the space beside that positive behavior remains empty. Reminding your child that she's losing the opportunity to earn stars can often motivate her to stop doing what you've established she shouldn't. Most children would much rather see stars or check marks instead of empty spaces. Especially when you begin your discipline plan, you may want to remind your child when she's losing her chance to earn a star or check mark. But remember that you should never take away a star or check mark once it's been earned. If she's earned it, it's hers to spend.

Let's look at how not earning check marks affected Jason Kim, the nine-year-old son of my clients Warren and Cordelia Kim.

Warren Kim shared this story of Jason's rude awakening to the reality of what not earning check marks meant. In a bad mood when he got home from school, Jason had spent the afternoon teasing his brother and goofing off in his room. As a result when he and his dad reviewed his chart right after dinner, Jason made an alarming discovery. He hadn't earned any check marks since breakfast. He didn't have enough to stay up and watch his favorite television show. He and his dad talked about how Jason would have to get busy if he wanted to watch his favorite show. Determined to fill up the empty spaces on his chart, Jason did his schoolwork, straightened up his room, and left his brother alone. This burst of energy was enough to earn him his favorite show. Jason promised his dad that he wouldn't wait until the last minute in the future. Although Jason's procrastination wasn't totally cured, as he played the Game he got much better about not putting things off until the last minute.

Using Warnings

Another technique you can use to help your child stop various kinds of problem behavior is a warning system. Warnings help your child become aware that he's behaving improperly and that you want him to stop. Warnings give your child a chance to think about what he's doing and stop doing it. When you use warnings as part of the total Behavior Game, they should help your child decrease his problem behavior. In fact, sometimes a warning can be enough to get your child to stop altogether. Here are some ways to make warnings work:

• **Deliver warnings in as calm and positive a manner as possible.** Although you may feel like screaming at your child to stop her problem behavior, try not to. Instead, take a deep breath, compose yourself, and, as calmly as you can, ask her to stop doing what she's doing.
• **Include a clear statement about what you want your child to stop doing and what will happen if he doesn't stop.**   For example, if he's bouncing a basketball on the kitchen floor, you might ask him to stop and let him know that if he doesn't he will not be able to play with the basketball for the

rest of the day. Or, if he's bothering you while you're trying to talk on the phone, you might suggest that he be quiet until you're finished or he'll have to go to his room for fifteen minutes.

• **Use only one warning.**   Warnings lose their effectiveness if you warn your child repeatedly to stop doing something. Warnings work only if your child believes that you intend to follow through with a consequence. If you use warnings over and over and don't follow through on the consequences, your child won't pay much attention to your warnings. She'll consider them meaningless because they're never enforced. If you use warnings without following up on the consequences, they won't help your child decrease her problem behavior. In fact, you'll be wasting your time. And you'll probably get pretty frustrated and angry as your child continues to ignore your warnings.

• **Don't make the consequences for not following a warning too severe.** As a consequence for not following a warning, choose a discipline technique that's fairly easy for you to deliver and that's enforceable. When a warning isn't followed, you can use one of the other discipline techniques described here, such as ignoring, time-out, quiet chair, or taking away a thing or a privilege for a short time. Do not combine a warning with a dire consequence that your child knows will never happen or that is so severe that you could not possibly carry it out; for example, "You'll never watch television again as long as you live." Warnings like this one will encourage your child to ignore any future warnings.

Let's see how my client Martha Goldstein used these ideas about giving warnings:

Before her family started playing the Behavior Game, Martha had often used warnings as empty threats of consequences that never happened. So no matter what she said, her daughters Rachel and Myria knew that she'd back down. She wouldn't take television away for a week and she'd never make them stay in their rooms until they could "act their age." But once Martha began sticking to her word and following warnings with consequences, things changed. For example, during a typically loud argument between Rachel and Myria over who was better at soccer, Martha asked the girls to tone it down or go to their rooms. Figuring she didn't really mean it, the girls kept arguing. Needless to say, they were quite surprised when Martha sent them to their rooms. Over time, as Martha followed through, the girls began to pay more attention to their mom because unlike before, Martha backed up her words and did what she said she was going to do.

Ignoring Irritating Behavior

Ignoring is another effective discipline technique for helping your child stop some of his irritating, attention-getting problem behavior. Some parents are surprised that I recommend ignoring as a discipline technique because when they tried it in the past it hasn't worked. However, the technique can be very effective if you make it part of your overall Behavior Game. It works because children often display annoying behavior to get a parent's attention. So when you ignore this behavior you are depriving your child of her reason for doing it. If your child whines, begs, or talks back in order to get your attention, she's likely to stop if you quit paying attention to her when she's acting that way.

Unfortunately, ignoring your child's irritating behavior is rarely easy. Problems such as bickering, arguing, begging, and mouthing off are usually hard to ignore because they get on your nerves. But before you rule out ignoring, give it a try by following these guidelines:

• **To decrease problem behavior, ignore it and reward its opposite. Never use ignoring without also using rewarding.**   You need to stop paying attention to your child's problem behavior while rewarding her good behavior. For example, you should try ignoring your child when she talks back or begs and try rewarding her for talking nicely and doing what you ask without a hassle.

• **Let your child know what he's doing that you don't like and that you're going to ignore him until he stops.**   When your child is begging, whining, or arguing, let him know that you don't like what he's doing and that you're not going to pay any attention to him until he stops. Then stick to your word and ignore him until he's stopped.

• **Don't look at your child, talk to him, or reason with him.**   Sometimes not paying attention to a problem behavior can seem almost impossible. You may find that ignoring is easier if you plan exactly what you're going to do while you try to ignore your child. You may want to be doing something such as reading a book or magazine, watching television, or performing a task—perhaps cleaning up the kitchen or folding laundry. You may need to leave the room while you're ignoring your child's behavior and come back only when she's stopped.

• **Even if the behavior temporarily gets worse, keep ignoring.** Sometimes your child's behavior gets worse, which is an unfortunate short-term effect of ignoring. When you start ignoring your child's problem behavior, he may try harder to get your attention by continuing longer, louder, harder, or more often. He may keep whining, refuse to stop arguing, beg nonstop, or talk back more.

Your child may be very persistent while she's trying to get your attention. If your child won't stop, and you reach a point where you just can't ignore her anymore, you can leave the room or send your child to her room.

• **Be prepared to hear how awful you are.** Your child is likely to let you know that he doesn't like being ignored. He may try to make you feel guilty and accuse you of not loving him, by saying something such as, "If you loved me, you'd care about me and pay attention to me." Keep in mind that you're ignoring your child's problem behavior, not the child himself. Try to ignore his "you don't love me" comments.

Let's see how these tips helped my client Joan Bradley use ignoring with her children Cindy and Bobby.

When Joan Bradley told me how much she'd like Cindy and Bobby to stop talking back to her, I suggested she consider ignoring this behavior. Joan was concerned that she wouldn't be able to ignore her children's obnoxious verbal behavior because it irritated her so much, especially if she'd have to sit silently and absorb their grating comments. I assured her that she didn't need to listen passively. Instead she should tell her children that she would ignore them until they had something nice to say. If necessary, she could leave the room and come back after they'd shaped up.

When Joan began ignoring Cindy and Bobby's back talk, they couldn't believe it. How could their mom treat them this way? Usually, if they persisted, she'd fight back. But now, it was as though she were deaf to their whining and name-calling. After a few days, as it sunk in that their mom wasn't going to pay attention to back talk, Cindy and Bobby became much more pleasant.

Although ignoring is effective, it won't work for every problem behavior. Ignoring will often help your child stop whining, pleading, begging, talking back, and arguing with you. However, your child will not be responsive:

• **If misbehaving is a lot of fun.**   If your child is having a great time playing in the mud in your backyard, ignoring will not make her stop.

• **If he is getting attention from other people, such as his brother, sister, or his friends.**   So long as your child is getting attention from someone, behavior such as arguing, teasing, bullying, name-calling, and fighting will continue.

• **If her behavior is dangerous.**   Obviously you don't want to ignore your child when she runs into the street, opens the medicine cabinet, or rides her bike without a helmet.

• **If he is getting out of something he doesn't want to do.**   If your child doesn't want to clean his room or finish his homework, ignoring won't get him to accomplish either task.

When ignoring doesn't work or if you just can't stand doing it anymore, you should consider using one of the discipline techniques described below. And no matter what discipline techniques you're using, always combine them with the Behavior Game and rewarding good behavior.

Time-Out

Time-out is sending your child to her room for a short amount of time as a consequence for misbehaving. Having time-out alone in her room and being quiet for five to ten minutes gives your child a chance to calm down and think about what she did. And, if you need it, this time also gives you a chance to regroup and get back in control.

Your child's room is usually the best place for time-out. Even though your child probably likes his room, it will work as a time-out room because you will be sending him there. If he's like most children he won't like having his parents send him to his room. And, of course, he won't be allowed to do fun things such as watch television, play video games, or listen to music.

If you can't use your child's room, pick another quiet, safe place. Never put your child in a place that is dark or scary. Never use a closet. Your child should not be afraid of the time-out room. The time-out room should be as quiet, neutral, and calm as possible. It should not frighten your child.

Whatever room you pick, be sure to remove anything valuable or dangerous. Some children may get destructive in time-out and break or ruin things. To prevent this, temporarily remove any items you're worried about. If your time-out room contains cupboards or closets, check the contents carefully and either lock the cupboards or remove anything that could be dangerous.

The way you put time-out into action determines how well it works. To make sure that time-out is effective, follow these steps:

•   **Give a warning before you put time-out into action.**   Let your child know that he's doing something you want him to stop and that he will have to take a time-out if he doesn't stop. Sometimes this will be enough and your child will stop misbehaving. However, other times your child may need something stronger, like time-out. Time-out works especially well with out-of-control behavior such as fighting, yelling, and tantrums.

•   **If your child continues misbehaving after you have warned her, send her to time-out.**   Let your child know that she's still acting improperly and that she must take a time-out. Be sure to follow through and send her to time-out. Make going to time-out very matter-of-fact. Don't discuss it. Don't reason or argue about it. Just send her to time-out as calmly and quickly as possible.

•   **Make your child stay in his room for time-out until he has been quiet for five to ten minutes.**   It's important that your child have a chance to calm down and get himself together. He needs at least five minutes of quiet time to do this. Don't let him leave the time-out room until he has had this opportunity to regroup.

•   **Ignore your child while she's in time-out unless you're concerned that she's hurt herself.**   If your child says horrible things to you while she's in time-out, try not to pay any attention. Some children get very angry when they're sent for time-out, especially the first few times, and say some pretty awful things. Unless your child is in danger or destroying something, ignore her.

Younger children may scream for a while in time-out and then fall asleep because they're exhausted. Unless you think your child has hurt himself, let him scream for a while and get it out of his system. For most parents, thirty minutes of screaming is enough. If your child has been screaming for thirty minutes, check to see that he is all right, and let your child know that if he keeps screaming you will take away a privilege or possession for a while. You might take away television for the rest of the day or take away a favorite toy or activity. *Don't take away his blanket or any toy that's a security item for him.*

• **Let your child know when time-out is over and that she can come out whenever she feels like it.**   Give your child a chance to leave the time-out room when she feels like it. Some children come out right away, others take a while.

• **When time-out is over, be nice to your child.**   Start over with a clean slate. Don't criticize him or get angry with him. He's served his time for misbehaving by going for a time-out. If you want, you can kindly let him know that you hope everyone can get along better so that no one will have to go back to time-out.

Let's see how my clients the Bradleys used time-out to help their children quit fighting with each other.

Although the Game had really helped Cindy and Bobby in a number of ways, it hadn't done much to improve their relationship with each other. They still fought like cats and dogs over the stupidest things such as who got to sit in the front seat, who was the best soccer player, who was the smartest. Whatever the topic, they could bicker and argue endlessly. Since Joan and Gary were pretty sure ignoring wouldn't work because the children enjoyed teasing each other so much, they decided to give them a warning and then, if the arguing didn't stop, send them for a time-out, each having to go to his or her own room and be quiet for ten minutes. Initially both children protested having to go for a time-out, but once they realized that time-out was going to happen no matter what they said, their objections decreased. After several weeks of going for time-out, Cindy and Bobby were arguing a lot less. And even though it was hard for both of them, Joan and Gary kept their promise to start with a clean slate when time-out was over rather than reviewing their children's misbehavior in detail. In fact, Cindy and Bobby told me how great it was that their parents weren't always bringing up all the bad things they'd done.

The Quiet Chair

If for whatever reason you don't want to use time-out, you can consider the "quiet chair." The quiet chair works like time-out, except that you have your child sit on a chair or in a corner instead of sending her to her room. The chair or corner should be in a quiet place away from the action. Your child should sit on the chair or in the corner quietly for five to ten minutes.

The quiet chair is not like a dunce chair. No one should ridicule your child or talk to him or make fun of him while he is sitting in the quiet chair. And, like time-out, going to the quiet chair or quiet corner should provide your child with the opportunity to calm down and think about what he has done. It also allows you to calm down.

You can put the quiet chair into action using the same steps you would use for time-out. Give a warning, and if that's not followed, send your child to the quiet chair. After she's been quiet for five to ten minutes, let her off the chair. Ignore her if she talks while she's sitting on the chair. If your child refuses to sit on the quiet chair or in the quiet corner, you can send her to her room for time-out.

Some families prefer a time-out, others prefer the quiet chair, and still others use a combination of time-out and the quiet chair. Use whatever works best for you.

Taking Away a Privilege or Possession

When you feel like you need something more than a time-out or the quiet chair, consider taking away a possession or privilege. This is often more effective with older children. Let's see how this technique works:

•   **When your child misuses one of his possessions, take it away from him for a short time.**   If your child misuses a toy or makes a mess with his crayons or markers, for example, you can take the offending item away for a while. You might also have him help you clean up the mess he made.

•   **When your child abuses a privilege, take that privilege away for a while.**   If your child is taking dangerous chances on her bike, you might want to take away bike privileges for several days. If she comes home late from a friend's house, you may want to take away her privilege of seeing friends for a day or two. If your child stays on the phone for hours, you can restrict phone privileges or take them away altogether for a few days.

• **Don't take away too much for too long.**   When your child does something you don't like and you're angry with him, it can be easy to fall into the trap of overdoing it and taking away too much. Even though you may feel like taking away everything your child owns for the rest of his life, don't do it; take away only one or two things for a short time. For example, if your child has not been doing his homework but instead has been listening to tapes and talking on the phone, even though you feel like ripping his phone out of the wall and pounding his tape player into pieces, try to calm down and come up with a plan that takes away his phone privileges and tape player for one to two days. Start small. You can always increase the amount of time that privileges are removed if you need to.

Let's see how my clients Nora and Darryl Hillman used these tips with their twelve-year-old daughter Penny:

Before playing the Game, Nora and Darryl fell into the trap of taking away a privilege for too long. When Penny came home from school late or did poorly on a test, she wasn't allowed to do anything or go anywhere for a week. As a result Penny spent a lot of time in her room, angry at her parents for being so mean. And she learned that if she complained enough, she could usually get her dad to back down and let her do something. So, instead of studying as her parents wanted her to, Penny spent a great deal of her time coming up with excuses for her behavior and reasons to let her out. Although she'd promise to try harder and be more responsible, in a day or two she'd fall into her old habits.

When her parents played the Game, not only did they set up a system to reward Penny for coming home on time and gradually improving at school, they also changed the manner in which they took away privileges. They reduced the punishment period from one to two weeks to one or two days. This combination proved very successful with Penny. She came home on time more often and spent more time on schoolwork. Of equal importance, her anger at her parents subsided because they weren't constantly confining her to her room.

You will notice that none of the discipline techniques I recommend involve getting tough with your child by using any kind of physical force or violence. Your discipline should *never* involve scaring or intimidating your child with threats of physical force, punishment, or violence, or actual physical force, punishment, or violence. Let's see why in the following discussion.

AVOIDING PHYSICAL PUNISHMENT, THREATS, AND INTIMIDATION

Physical punishment or even threats of physical punishment can be dangerous to your child and should *never* be used to get any kind of problem behavior under control. Do not hit or spank your child to get her to stop doing something. Do not threaten your child with possible spankings or beatings when she's being bad. No matter how angry you are, avoid getting physically tough when you discipline your child.

Parents usually resort to getting tough only when they don't know what else to do and everything they've tried has failed. In their desperation, they may start spanking harder and longer; they may put children on long, severe restrictions; they may bully their children and attempt to scare them. They may try to get even with their children. None of these get-tough techniques is effective and each is very damaging for a number of reasons.

Many kinds of problem behavior can increase and intensify when overly tough discipline is used. When parents use severe punishments, they may anger their child so much that he will retaliate and act even worse. A power struggle can develop in which the child and the parents act increasingly harshly toward one another, and the child's bad behavior actually gets worse.

When parents get tough with punishments, they run the risk of alienating their child. Their child may start to dislike, fear, and avoid her parents. She may withdraw or become rebellious. It can become harder to communicate with her. By the time their child is an adolescent, she may be very unhappy, unreachable, and unmanageable. When this happens, the parent-child relationship can be damaged permanently.

I've never worked with a family where getting tough did anything good for anyone. Let's take a minute to look firsthand at what happened to my clients Giselle and Keith Burton when they tried to knuckle down and get tough with their son Danny.

When the Burtons first visited me, they were worried that their eleven-year-old son Danny would never behave better. They felt as though they had tried everything and nothing, not even getting tough, had worked. He was still acting up, getting in fights, talking back, and coming home late. Since none of their efforts had been effective, the Burtons wondered if it was time to start using physical punishment with Danny. Before cautioning them about the many problems that physical punishment can cause, I asked them to describe what techniques they had used with Danny.

Worried they had been too lenient with their son, Giselle and Keith initiated a program to get Danny to shape up by letting him know everything wrong with what he was doing. They made sure to lecture him frequently about how he should grow up and take more responsibility for his behavior. When he did something wrong they were quick to criticize and punish him by making him spend the weekends at home away from friends. Often they took his allowance away as well.

In spite of their efforts, Danny's behavior didn't get better. In fact, it got worse, and he became even more distant, unhappy, angry, and argumentative. When he was sent to his room for the afternoon, he didn't seem to care. He'd shut the door and disappear. He seemed immune to his parents' yelling and criticizing. It was as if everything Giselle and Keith said went in one ear and out the other. Danny seemed to be avoiding his parents whenever possible.

I could see that Danny was at a loss. He didn't know what to do to please his parents, so he had given up trying. When I talked with Danny, he told me that he was tired of hearing about all the bad things he did. It seemed as though all he ever did was cause trouble. When he tried to be good, it didn't work. He always messed up. Sometimes he wanted to run away from home. No matter what he did he seemed to get punished. His parents never noticed when he tried to be good.

Even though Giselle and Keith thought they were doing the right thing and that getting tough would help Danny shape up and act better, it had had the opposite effect. To help Danny, the Burtons needed to change their approach. They needed to begin using the Behavior Game and rewarding Danny's good behavior. Although skeptical, the Burtons agreed to give the Game a try.

On his next visit Danny told me how surprised he'd been when his parents started rewarding him and putting check marks on a Good Behavior Chart. Although he kept waiting for his parents to punish him for not being perfect, to erase check marks off his chart, or to cancel the Game when he slipped up, it never happened. Instead, when he misbehaved his parents only sent him to his room until he "could get it together." He told me that although he didn't like time-out, it was certainly better than what his parents had done before. And, most important, he confided in me that he really liked earning rewards and getting compliments. He decided maybe his parents weren't so bad after all. Giselle and Keith were equally pleased. After only a few weeks with the Behavior Game, they couldn't help but notice how much better Danny's behavior and attitude were.

YOUR DISCIPLINE PLAN

Using a Discipline Plan form, you can combine the techniques you just read about into a plan of action. (See sample form on next page.)

As you make up your discipline plan, keep these two rules in mind:

• **Keep using the Game.** Always use your discipline plan and the Behavior Game together, never use your discipline plan alone. Whenever possible, reward good behavior that is the opposite of problem behavior.
• **Make up a plan that uses warnings and ignoring first.** In your plan include time-out, the quiet chair, and/or taking away a privilege or possession for those times when warnings and ignoring aren't enough.

To Do

1. *Copy:* Make a copy of the Discipline Plan form for each child who's participating in the Game. You'll find this form in Appendix A.
2. *Fill out:* As you fill out a Discipline Plan form for each child, refer to the problem scenarios below for tips on which discipline techniques to use.
3. *Save:* Keep your plan in a private but easy-to-find place so that you can refer to it when your child misbehaves.

Let's take a look at some ways to use a combination of discipline techniques effectively in the following situations.

Discipline Plan

For _____

Instructions: Put a check beside each problem your child continues to have, and then fill in which discipline techniques you plan to use. Be sure to consider warnings, ignoring, time-out, the quiet chair, and taking away a privilege or possession for a short time.

☐ Not getting up on time
☐ Not getting dressed without a hassle
☐ Not taking care of self
☐ Not eating breakfast nicely
☐ Not being ready for school on time
☐ Not getting along with brothers/sisters
☐ Not getting along with friends
☐ Not getting along with parents
☐ Not doing what is asked
☐ Not doing chores
☐ Not doing schoolwork
☐ Not eating dinner nicely
☐ Not getting ready for bed
☐ Not going to bed
☐ Not staying in bed
☐ Other

• **If your child continues to have problems getting up in the morning, getting ready for school, and eating breakfast nicely:** Continue playing the Game, allowing your child to earn rewards for doing well. This technique may be enough to get her to improve dramatically. It may help to remind your child that she'll lose out on earning stars if she doesn't behave in accordance with her chart. Try to ignore the whining, complaining, and other irritating kinds of behavior that often accompany getting up in the morning and getting ready for school. If things are going poorly, you may need to take away a favorite before-school activity, such as watching cartoons or playing a game.

• **If your child is having trouble getting along with other children:** When your children are arguing but not trying to hurt one another, let them know you're going to ignore them until they can get along. Sometimes your ignoring will be enough to get your children to quit their arguing, teasing, or whatever they're doing. However, often it's not enough because your children are getting too much attention from one another. If ignoring doesn't work to stop a minor disagreement and/or their arguing keeps getting worse, use time-out or the quiet chair.

When your children are hurting one another, warn them to stop immediately. If that doesn't work, put time-out or the quiet chair into action.

It's usually best to send everyone involved in an argument for a time-out or to the quiet chair. In most cases it doesn't matter who started the argument or the fight; whoever is participating in it should go for a time-out. Put your children in separate rooms or in separate quiet chairs. If you only want to send one child at a time for a time-out, you can alternate who goes. When in doubt send the older one; it may not be fair, but the older one should have more responsibility to see that fights are stopped or don't get worse.

When your child has a spat with a friend, ignore it if it's a minor squabble. If possible, it's always a good idea to let friends try to work out their differences on their own. However, if this approach doesn't work and the arguing gets worse, you can send your child for a time-out, and if you have his parents' permission, you can also send his friend for a time-out or to the quiet chair. If the arguing still keeps getting worse, send the friend home or take away the privilege of having a friend over or going to a friend's house for a day or two.

• **If your child isn't getting along with you:**   When your child whines or begs or talks back, let her know you're going to ignore her until she stops. Over time, your ignoring may help your child stop behaving in these irritating ways. However, many parents can stand to ignore this kind of grating behavior for only so long. If your child keeps at it and you can't ignore her anymore, you can send her for a time-out or to the quiet chair. Also, if you feel that your child's comments are getting too disrespectful or disobedient for you to ignore, let her know how you feel and then send her for a time-out. Being in her room gives her a chance to think about what she has been saying, and how it's affecting other people's feelings. It also gives you a chance to calm down.

When you see a tantrum starting, give your child a warning that time-out is right around the corner. If your child continues his screaming and crying, send him for the time-out.

- **If your child doesn't do what you ask:**   When your child ignores your requests, promises to do something but doesn't follow through, or simply refuses, remind her that she is losing out on stars by not doing what you ask. If that's not enough to get her to go along with your wishes, give your child a warning and if necessary send her for a time-out. If a time-out isn't enough, you may also need to take away a privilege or possession.

- **If your child is having problems doing chores:**   Make sure that your child understands exactly what you want him to do and that he knows how to do it. After you've determined that he knows how to do the chore but is refusing to do it, give him a warning that a time-out is in the near future. If the warning doesn't work, follow through with a time-out. If this fails as well, use a loss of privilege or possession for a short time.

- **If your child is having problems doing homework:**   Make sure the study periods you're giving are short enough. You may need to reduce study time to smaller increments, for example, give ten minutes of study instead of fifteen. Remind your child that she can earn check marks. Consider a special reward that can only be earned by doing schoolwork. When that's not enough you may need to adopt a system of giving a warning, and then if necessary sending your child for a time-out or taking away a privilege. Keep in mind that if your child hates doing homework, she may prefer having a time-out to studying. If so, taking away a privilege like playing video games or watching television may be more effective.

- **If your child has problems eating dinner nicely:**   If your child isn't eating his food or is bothering the family at dinnertime, a combination of warnings, some ignoring until you can't stand it, and time-out usually works well. You can let him finish dinner after he's done with his time-out.

- **If your child has problems getting ready for bed:**   If your child is taking forever to get ready for bed, she may need to start getting ready earlier. You may also want to use a reminder that she is not earning stars and may not have time to enjoy her before-bed reward, whether it's reading a story or staying up an extra 30 minutes. This kind of reminder should help her speed things up. Using a time-out or the quiet chair usually doesn't work very well with bedtime behavior, because these techniques take up time and further delay getting ready for bed.

- **If your child has problems going to bed or staying in bed:**   These can be two of the toughest problems that parents have to deal with. Many children don't want to go to bed, so they come up with reason after reason why they can't go to bed yet. As hard as it is, you've got to be firm and unyielding. If your child is refusing to go to bed or stay in bed, remind him that he's not earning stars and ignore his protests as much as you can. If he just won't stop, consider taking away a privilege such as riding his bike or playing video games for a day.

When you've finished making up your discipline plan, it's time to put it into practice in combination with your child's Game. As described below, there's an art to introducing discipline and the idea of problem behavior to your children.

PUTTING YOUR PLAN INTO ACTION

Since children are rarely thrilled about the prospect of any kind of discipline, it's a good idea to be thoroughly prepared before you put your plan into action. If necessary take an extra day or two to think about your plan and make sure you're clear about what you're going to do.

Keep in mind that no matter how diplomatically you present your discipline plan and in spite of whatever positive spin you put on it, your children are not likely to embrace it with open arms. They won't like hearing about their problems or how you plan to deal with them. They won't want to think about things like being ignored, going for a time-out, or not getting to do something they want to do. They'd rather concentrate on earning stars and check marks and getting rewards, and forget about their so-called problems. Cindy and Bobby Bradley were no exception. Let's look in on the Bradleys as Gary and Joan explain their discipline plan to Bobby and Cindy. (Copies of their discipline plans are provided on the following pages.)

After playing the Behavior Game for a week, Cindy and Bobby were raring to go and start another week. They had many things they wanted to buy with the money they were earning, and Cindy had already planned what she would do during the extra half hour she got to stay up. So when the family sat down to talk about their Games for the next week, imagine

Cindy's and Bobby's surprise when their parents started talking about their problem behavior.

After letting Cindy and Bobby know how pleased he was with all their progress, their dad started talking about how they still had some problems, such as having tantrums when they didn't get their way and refusing to do what they were asked. Cindy, in particular, felt that her dad was making a big deal about nothing. Sure, sometimes she got upset and screamed and cried—who didn't? And, sometimes when her parents asked her to do something she didn't want to do she refused. They just needed to quit asking her to do such stupid stuff—that's all it would take. But her dad simply kept talking.

All of a sudden their dad was describing something called time-out, where they'd be sent to their rooms and stay there until they'd been quiet for five minutes. Cindy thought that sounded like a stupid idea. She told her dad she didn't want to go for a time-out and that something that stupid wouldn't help. Her dad said he was sorry she didn't like the idea, but she'd have to go anyway. Bobby didn't think it sounded like much fun either. But neither Bobby nor Cindy was worried. Somehow, they'd find a way to avoid a time-out. They'd never have to go for a time-out. It was just talk.

Introducing Your Discipline Plan

Most families find that it works best to introduce their discipline plan at the same time they're starting the Game for a new week. Here are some ideas to help you put a positive spin on your discipline plan.

• **Get the whole family together for your regular weekly meeting on Sunday and begin by talking about how well things have been going.** Review how well your child is doing. Let her know how pleased you are and how much you're looking forward to the next week and all the stars and check marks she will be earning for all her good behaviors.

• **After this positive introduction, add that there is still room for improvement on everyone's part.** Let your child know that even though many good things have happened, you feel like there still are some improvements the family can make.

Discipline Plan

For *Cindy Bradley*

Instructions: Put a check beside each problem your child continues to have, and then fill in which discipline techniques you plan to use. Be sure to consider warnings, ignoring, time-out, the quiet chair, and taking away a privilege or possession for a short time. *Keep this private!* A lot of improvement, but *don't let up and keep the following in mind when problems happen:*

☑	Not getting up on time *if not up after one reminder won't earn* ✓
☐	Not getting dressed without a hassle *not a problem, a reminder and ✓ should do it*
☐	Not taking care of self *not much difficulty here; may need reminder to hurry up occasionally*
☑	Not eating breakfast nicely *reminder, ✓; ignore minor offenses, send for time-out if needed*
☐	Not being ready for school on time *pretty good about, always give ✓*
☑	Not getting along with brothers/sisters *one warning, try to ignore, if can't ignore, send for time-out*
☑	Not getting along with friends *one warning, encourage them to work out; if can't, time-out/send home*
☑	Not getting along with parents *especially Mom; warn, ignore, leave room, if can't stand, use time-out*
☑	Not doing what is asked *warning and time-out, take away privilege if needed, stay on top of this*
☐	Not doing chores *doing much better, ✓ seems to help, continue ✓ and praise*
☐	Not doing schoolwork *doing better, continue short time periods and frequent breaks and ✓*
☑	Not eating dinner nicely *remind, ignore minor things, send for time-out if needed*
☑	Not getting ready for bed *reward of staying up later seems to help her get ready for bed. whew!*
☑	Not going to bed *much more willing to go to bed after staying up—wonderful!*
☐	Not staying in bed *must be too tired to argue about this*
☐	Other

Discipline Plan

For _Bobby Bradley_

Instructions: Put a check beside each problem your child continues to have, and then fill in which discipline techniques you plan to use. Be sure to consider warnings, ignoring, time-out, the quiet chair, and taking away a privilege or possession for a short time. _Keep this private!_ _A lot of improvement, but don't let up and keep the following in mind when problems happen:_

☑	Not getting up on time _always expect to remind and encourage, ✓ is very important_
☑	Not getting dressed without a hassle _ignore small stuff, help out, be patient, give two ✓_
☑	Not taking care of self _be patient, remind, help out, let him do as much as he can, two ✓_
☑	Not eating breakfast nicely _reminder, ✓; ignore minor offenses, send for time-out if needed_
☐	Not being ready for school on time _pretty good about, always give ✓_
☑	Not getting along with brothers/sisters _one warning, try to ignore, if can't ignore, send for time-out_
☑	Not getting along with friends _one warning, encourage them to work out; if can't, time-out/send home_
☑	Not getting along with parents _warn, ignore, leave room; if can't stand use time-out_
☑	Not doing what is asked _warning and time-out, take away privilege if needed; not as bad as Cindy_
☑	Not doing chores _doing much better, ✓ seems to help, continue ✓ and praise_
☑	Not doing schoolwork _doing better, continue short time periods and frequent breaks and ✓_
☑	Not eating dinner nicely _remind, ignore minor things, send for time-out if needed_
☑	Not getting ready for bed _reward of story or staying up later seems to help him get ready for bed_
☑	Not going to bed _much more willing to go to bed after story or staying up— wonderful!_
☐	Not staying in bed _must be too tired to argue about this_
☐	Other

• **Give your child examples of how you're trying to do better at the Game.**   Telling your child that you have some problems you're still striving to correct can be extremely effective in getting him to accept that he too may have some things to work on. Telling him about improvements you're trying to make lets him know that no one is perfect, even his own parents. For instance, you might explain to him that you're trying to do a better job of playing the Game by noticing more good things that he is doing, or by not yelling so much, or by listening more. Whatever you're working on, talk to your child about it.

• **Give your child examples of things you'd like her to work on.**   Mention the behaviors that she needs to work on most. Don't mention every little thing she does that gets on your nerves. Be brief. Concentrate only on the most important problem behavior. Perhaps she is having trouble getting along and doing what you ask. Or maybe she's having difficulty getting her homework done or getting up on time or going to bed on time.

• **Avoid using the words** *discipline plan.*   Just like Gary Bradley you should not mention the word *discipline*. Most children zone out when they hear that word. Instead, focus on specific behavior you want your child to change and *on your response.* Let your child know that *you're* going to do things differently when these problems occur. Since what you've done in the past, such as yelling or arguing or whatever it was, hasn't worked very well, explain that you're going to try some new things.

• **Give your child some examples of what you plan to do.**   Go over the behavior problems you want to change and tell your child what you plan to do when each one happens. Let him know that first you'll give him a warning by asking him to stop whatever he's doing. If that doesn't work you'll try one of the following: ignoring, time-out, the quiet chair, or taking away a privilege or possession.

• **Give a quick example of what you mean by ignoring, time-out, the quiet chair, and taking away a privilege.**   You might describe how you plan to ignore your child's whining or begging or whatever else she does that gets on your nerves. Or you can fill her in on your plans to send her to her room for time-out when she can't stop arguing with or teasing her brother. Make sure she understands that she'll need to be quiet in her room for five to ten minutes before she'll be allowed to leave. If you plan to use the quiet chair, give her an example of how it will work. You may want to let her know that sometimes when things aren't going well, like in the morning when she's not getting ready, she won't get to do something she enjoys, such as watching television or playing a video game.

• **No matter how poor a reception your plan gets, don't worry, it can still work.** Your child may deny that he has any problems or assert that the problems you're describing aren't his fault. He may insist that he doesn't need things like time-out and/or that he can stop doing everything you're talking about on his own without being ignored or sent to his room. Regardless of your child's objections, do not waver; put your plan into action.

• **Switch gears and concentrate on the positive aspects of the Game.** At this point your child is likely to be sick of hearing about time-out, the quiet chair, and all her so-called problem behavior. So wrap up the discussion by stressing how everyone will be working together during the coming week. And remember, your children actually need to experience time-out and everything else you've just talked about before they can really understand what you mean.

• **Get the Game started again.** Once you've finished introducing your plan, follow the same eight steps you do every week to get the Game going again. As a reminder, these are listed at the end of chapter 4.

Sticking to Your Plan

When you first put your discipline plan into action, expect a challenge to your ideas. Don't be surprised by the lengths your child may go to as she tries to persuade you that your plan stinks, it's not needed, and it won't work.

Expect your child to test the limits to see if you really mean what you said. Your child may act up on purpose to find out. Will you really send him for a time-out if he plays rough with his sister or if he refuses to eat dinner? Will you really take his bike away if he forgets to wear his helmet? Will you keep the television turned off if he's not making progress on his homework? You need to be on your toes and ready to put your discipline plan into action at a moment's notice.

Let's look in on the Bradleys at this stage:

Gary decided that doing some yard work would be a great way for Cindy and Bobby to earn some money. Neither child was enthusiastic about the idea. Bobby wanted to play a favorite video game and Cindy wanted to ride bikes with her friend Ellen.

In the past Gary would have let both of them do what they wanted and done the yard work himself, but not today. Gary told Cindy and Bobby they could do what they wanted after they helped him with the yard work.

Bobby and Cindy didn't want to wait. Cindy started arguing about how she never got to play with Ellen and that Ellen was counting on her to come over. Bobby sulked and refused to come outside.

Gary calmed himself down, restrained himself from yelling, and let his children know that if they didn't start helping him right away he'd send them to their rooms for time-outs. Cindy couldn't believe her ears— all she wanted to do was to see Ellen. Boy, was her dad overreacting. If she could just reason with him, surely he'd understand and let her go. "Come on, Dad. All I ever do around here is work, work, work. I'm taking a break and going to Ellen's."

Instead of giving in, Gary sent Cindy to her room for a time-out. As her dad led her off to her room, Cindy started screaming. She couldn't believe it. Time-out? He had to be kidding. Gary put her in her room and closed the door. Cindy was furious and kept yelling about how unfair this was. No one paid any attention. No one even told her to be quiet.

Bobby, seeing what had happened to Cindy, decided it would be a good idea to help his dad and avoid the time-out. Eventually, Cindy got tired of screaming and sat down on her bed and thought about how much she didn't like being sent to her room. Finally, her dad came to the door and asked if she was ready to help him with the yard work. Reluctantly she said, "I guess so."

As Gary, Bobby, and Cindy cleaned up the yard, Cindy forgot about how upset she had been and actually helped her dad and brother. When they finished it was too late to ride bikes, but Cindy didn't seem to mind. Joan and Gary were surprised that Cindy was in a good mood for the remainder of the day. They had been concerned that she might be resentful about having to go for a time-out and take it out on them, but instead she got along pretty well with everyone.

Just as Gary did, when a specific problem behavior occurs, follow through and stick to your plan. If your plan says that you'll use a time-out for rough behavior, when your child uses rough behavior and a warning isn't enough, send her to her room. If she says she's sorry and she'll never do it again, she still gets sent to her room. No matter how many apologies your child makes, *if she doesn't respond to your warning, she has to experience the consequences.* She has to go for a time-out.

Be warned that no matter how careful you were in making up your discipline plan, your child may accuse you of being unfair and mean. Most children dislike being disciplined and may share their displeasure with you by saying nasty things and accusing you of not loving them. If this happens, try to ignore their remarks and give them and yourself a chance to calm down.

Most parents don't like having their child get angry at them; however, there's no way around it. Enforcing discipline techniques and listening to your child rant and rave is upsetting. But be prepared for it; in fact, expect it. In time, your child will stop lashing out. But for now, statements such as, "I don't love you," or "How could you do this to me? It's not my fault" are to be expected. Try to stay calm and ignore these outbreaks. If you feel your child is going too far with his verbal abuse, warn him and send him for a time-out until he gets control of himself.

Above all, do not abandon your discipline plan, even when your child is starting to get to you with her claims of unfair treatment and her accusations that you are an un-loving monster. If you give in and decide she doesn't have to go for a time-out "just this once," or that you're not going to take away her bike privileges "this time," you're teaching your child that she doesn't need to take you seriously and that she can get whatever she wants if she is persistent enough.

Give your child and yourself time to get used to your plan. After a few weeks, most children, even the most belligerent, adjust to discipline techniques such as time-out or the quiet chair. Try to be patient if your child is initially resistant to your plan.

Keep your plan in a private place. The form itself is an organizational tool for you—and a reminder of how you've decided to react when your kids begin driving you crazy.

Adding to Your Plan

Give your plan a week or two before you make any changes. Breaking bad habits can take a long time. It can take two, three, four, or even more weeks for your child to show improvement. And keep in mind that although your child's problems will get better, they may never go away completely. Your children will never get along perfectly all the time. And you will hear begging and whining from time to time no matter how successful your Game is.

If your lack of progress is getting you down and you feel as if you need something more, consider adding to your discipline plan in the following ways:

• **Make time-out longer.**   Sometimes, with older children in particular, parents find that time-out doesn't seem to be helping problem behavior decrease. If you're using time-out frequently for problems but it isn't helping, consider lengthening the time your child needs to spend in time-out to fifteen, twenty, or thirty minutes. You may find that these longer time-outs are much more effective.

• **Make time-out boring.**   Double-check that your child is not having fun during a time-out. Time-outs won't work if your child is watching television, listening to music, or talking on the phone. If you need to, remove these fun things from his room until he can be in a time-out without having access to them.

• **If neither of these changes seem to help, consider using restriction.** Restriction is keeping your child in the house for a certain period of time. It's like a long time-out in which more things are taken away. Restriction is usually reserved for older children and for serious problem behavior. For example, if your child is careless and almost starts a fire, if he or she gets in a bad fight at school, if she does poorly on a test because she didn't study for it, if she comes home very late and has worried you, if she tells a big lie, or if she does something that infuriates you—these are the times to think about using restriction. During restriction you can limit or prohibit leaving the house, watching television, making phone calls, and listening to music.

When thinking about a restriction, it's a good idea to send your child to his room while you're trying to decide what consequence he should get for misbehaving. Try to calm down and think rationally about what an appropriate consequence is. Here are some ways to make restrictions work:

Use restriction infrequently and only for serious problem behavior.   If you give your child a restriction every time he does something wrong, restriction will lose its effectiveness and you'll end up having to deal with an angry child who's always confined to the house. Many problems will go away without having to invoke a restriction, so save this technique as a last resort when nothing else works.

Consider a restriction if your child does something dangerous or harmful. In this case, of course, stop the behavior right away, explain why it is dangerous or harmful, and decide on a consequence. You may want to use a short restriction. For example, if your child runs into the street, you may want to keep her in the house for a while before she's allowed to play again. You can also make "staying out of the street" a good behavior on his chart. Try to set up a plan that discourages dangerous or harmful behavior by rewarding its opposite.

Children also need immediate consequences for behavior that hurts others. Separation and time-out or restriction can usually help decrease play that is too rough.

Make the restriction last for a short time, such as one or two days, not one or two weeks. Parents often overreact when they give their child a restriction. They may be angry and hand down a harsh, overly long penalty. Shorter restrictions can work as well as, and sometimes better than, long restrictions. Perhaps the worst part about a long restriction is that you have a miserable, angry child in your house all the time, and you have to deal with him. In this kind of situation, one has to wonder, who's really being punished—you or your child?

If you overreact, calm down, and then consider a less severe restriction. If in the heat of the moment you decide to take everything away from your child or put your child on a month-long restriction, regroup, rethink this kind of excessive restriction, and come up with something milder. Explain to your child that you were upset and angry and overreacted and that you've come up with a better, fairer restriction. As a rule, it's good to try to calm yourself down before you decide on a restriction. That way you're more likely to come up with something reasonable that you won't have to change later.

Since in this chapter it was impossible to cover every problem you may encounter, you may find it helpful to refer to Appendix B for additional references on using discipline techniques in a variety of situations.

Once you're comfortable using your discipline plan with your child, you're ready to move on to the next chapter and find out how to raise your expectations for your child's behavior gradually, how to take the Game on the road, and how to get other adults in your child's life involved in the Behavior Game.

6

RAISING EXPECTATIONS AND INVOLVING OTHER ADULTS

In this chapter you'll discover ways you expand the scope of your Behavior Game. First, you'll find some suggestions on how to raise the standards for your child's behavior. Next, you'll learn how to take the Game on the road when you're out with your child. And since the Game works even better if other adult caregivers are involved, you'll also learn about how to encourage another parent, your child's baby-sitter, and, if necessary, even a teacher to participate.

MAKING CHANGES IN THE GAME

As the weeks go by and your child is improving, you may want to consider refining the Behavior Game. However, be sure not to rush yourself or your child; take your time and consider various ideas that may occur to you. There are no set rules about making changes. You may or may not want to incorporate any of the following suggestions. Do whatever feels most comfortable for you and your child. Remember if you make a change that doesn't work out you can always return to the original Game.

Cutting Back on Advance Notices, Reminders, and Direct Assistance

Once your child gets in the habit of good behavior, you may not need to remind her as much. In fact, gradually decreasing the reminders you give her will help her learn to do things on her own. This technique works well with older children who can remember a series of things they're supposed to do. Consider the case of my clients the Jeffersons.

Since ten-year-old Tina Jefferson had so much difficulty remembering to do what she was supposed to do, when the family first started playing the Game, her mom, Grace, decided to remind her separately about each good behavior on her chart. Then after several weeks, as Tina started getting the hang of the Game, Grace began reminding her of several things simultaneously. For example, in the morning after Tina got up, her mom reviewed everything she needed to do before coming to breakfast: get dressed, brush her teeth, wash her face, comb her hair, go to the bathroom, and wash her hands before coming to the table for breakfast. At breakfast Grace let Tina know that when she'd finished eating, she needed to put her lunch and homework in her backpack and then put on her jacket. Tina's mom was so pleased with how well this plan worked that she used the same technique in the afternoon and evening. Eventually Tina was able to rattle off everything she was supposed to do on her own.

Once you feel your child is ready, you can use this type of general reminder throughout the day. You can set the stage by giving an overview of what needs to get done in the morning, the afternoon, and the evening. Eventually, by using this process you'll help your child remember bigger and bigger chunks of what he's supposed to do. He'll need fewer and fewer reminders. In fact, in time he'll be able to do most, if not all, of what you want him to do with almost no reminders. And, he'll be able to tell you what you expect of him. Keep in mind that younger children often won't remember as much as their older brothers or sisters will. For them, you'll have to cut back on reminders more slowly.

Your child may always need reminders about those things he especially dislikes doing. Even though you're providing rewards, you may need to remind him about certain good behavior such as cleaning his room, starting his homework, or going to bed on time.

Let's see how my client Florence Jacobs used this idea to help her daughter Mary clean her room.

Mary, age ten, was doing well with her Behavior Game except that she really hated to clean her room. She didn't mind if it looked like a pigsty. As she delighted in telling her mom, she knew where everything was and wasn't that what mattered? Although she wished that Mary would take care of her room like her sister Judy did, Florence was realistic. It was unlikely that Mary would ever have a "really neat and tidy" room, but still some improvement was necessary. Among other things, dirty clothes needed to go in the hamper, and the toys and books that were scattered around the room needed to be put away. Although rewarding Mary helped, she still was likely to forget when it came time to clean her room. For the moment, Florence decided that if she wanted Mary to clean her room, she'd need to remind her every day when she got home from school. Fortunately using both reminders and rewards was an effective combination, and Mary's room improved dramatically.

Sometimes, whether you like it or not, the reality is that if you want your child to do something, you'll need to remind her as well as reward her. So it's a good idea to be prepared to use reminders for hard-to-change behavior for a long, long time.

As your child improves his behavior, gradually decrease the direct assistance you're giving him for certain good behavior, such as getting up, getting dressed, brushing his teeth, washing his face, combing his hair, and/or getting ready for bed. Again, a gradual tapering off is recommended.

A younger child will need your help until she is actually capable of doing these things by herself. She's likely to let you know when she's ready to try things on her own. Give her an opportunity to "do it herself," and be there to offer support when needed.

Increasing Amounts of Time Required for Good Behavior

If your child is getting along better with others, you can gradually increase the number of minutes he needs to maintain the behavior in order to earn a star or check mark. Let's see how this suggestion worked for my clients the Ursich family.

After a few weeks of playing the Game, Valde and Misha couldn't believe it—sometimes their sons Ben, age six, and Randy, age eight, were actually able to get along for fifteen minutes and each earn a star. This was a big change from the constant warfare that existed before the Behavior Game.

Although they were tempted to increase time limits radically, as we talked about it, Valde and Misha decided to go slowly and try doubling the time limit to thirty minutes. This worked so well that several weeks later they increased the amount of time to an hour. Unfortunately, this last change was asking too much of their sons. After a few days they realized that an hour was too long. Their sons couldn't go for more than forty minutes without beginning to fight. After they scaled back the time to thirty minutes, Ben and Randy were able to earn stars again. So, at least for a while longer, they wouldn't exceed the thirty-minute time limit.

When your child is ready, you can try lengthening her "getting along" time and see how it works. As a rule, have at least three "getting along" times during the day. Many families find that using morning, afternoon, and evening time works well. Whenever you increase a time limit, always make sure your child understands that you're making the change because she's improving.

Using Caution Where Schoolwork Is Concerned

Most families I work with find that getting children to do schoolwork isn't easy. So even after your child is improving with his schoolwork, you may want to keep the same time limits. And, unless you have an older child, don't use a time limit of over fifteen minutes. Almost without exception, when families I've worked with have tried to increase study time to thirty minutes or one hour, it hasn't worked. Their children have rebelled and their performance deteriorated. Continue rewarding fifteen-minute periods of doing schoolwork, and if your child still isn't finishing his homework, consider providing him with a reward that can be earned only when he finishes all the schoolwork he's been assigned.

Let's see how my clients the Emersons used a special reward to help their daughter.

For Sarah, age eleven, sitting down and doing her homework continued to be a struggle. Although she was able to accomplish all the other good behavior her parents, Jane and Stan, wanted and thus earn a lot of stars, she found finishing her schoolwork, reading, or studying for a test a challenge. To help motivate her, Jane allowed Sarah to stay up later and watch her favorite television show only if she had completed all her schoolwork. Every day when Sarah got home from school, she and her mom mapped out what needed to be done and came up with a schedule. For each fifteen minutes of studying, Sarah could earn a check mark, and once she had finished everything, she could earn the privilege of staying up thirty minutes later to see her show. After a few days this special reward seemed to be just what Sarah needed to help her get her schoolwork done. In fact, every day when she got home from school, Sarah would look through the television listings and decide what she would watch before bed.

Adding On to Chores

If your child is doing well with a chore, you may want add a new task. But make these changes one task at a time, as my clients the Martins did.

History was being made when Joel, age seven, and resident slob of the Martin household, was actually putting his dirty clothes in the hamper and picking up his toys. Buoyed by their success, his parents, Ruth and Tad, were tempted to add all kinds of tasks for Joel to do. However, using restraint they chose only one additional task—putting his clean clothes in his drawers. After a few days of reminders and encouragement, Joel started earning stars for putting his clothes away. Ruth and Tad waited a week to add any additional tasks. There would be plenty of time in the future to include making his bed, cleaning up after himself in the bathroom, and feeding the dog.

Always add one task at a time and always show your child exactly what you want her to do and reward her for trying to do it. Furthermore, no matter how well your child is doing, it's not wise to require more than three chores per day, especially if each chore (such as cleaning one's room or helping with dinner) requires a series of tasks. If you do add tasks to your child's chores, let her know that it's because she's improving and showing responsibility. In addition, you may want to increase the number of stars or check marks your child can earn when you add tasks or make them more demanding.

Limiting the Number of Stars or Check Marks
Good Behavior Can Earn

Not often, but every now and then, one of my clients finds that their child performs a certain good behavior repeatedly in order to earn a lot of stars. Let's see what steps the Wongs took when this happened with their son Ted.

Although Ted was only six, he quickly figured out that each time he volunteered to help, he got a star on his chart. Most days he earned so many stars for helping out that he wasn't motivated to earn stars for other things his parents wanted him to do, such as getting ready for bed and going to bed. He didn't need any additional stars to buy the rewards he wanted. His mom and dad, Alice and John, solved this problem by putting an upper limit of ten stars Ted could earn each day for "doing what is asked." Now to get all the rewards he wants, Ted needs to perform other kinds of good behavior as well.

Like the Wongs did, you may want to set a limit of ten stars per day for doing what is asked or offering to help. I don't recommend that you use this kind of limit on behavior such as doing schoolwork or getting along with brothers and sisters because it can be appropriate to earn more than ten check marks per day for these kinds of often difficult behavior.

Remember, your child's earning too many stars or check marks is a much better situation than her earning too few. So don't be concerned about too many stars unless your child is earning so many that he's losing interest in the Game. Most children stay interested in the Game no matter how many stars they're earning. This was certainly true for my clients Elaine and Roger Johnson.

Eleven-year-old Tom Johnson had always liked to save up for things, and now, with playing the Game, the sky was the limit. Every day he traded in ten check marks for the privilege of staying up an extra thirty minutes. He converted all the other check marks he'd earned into money, which he immediately put into his secret bank. Even though some days he'd earn more than fifty check marks, he didn't lose interest in the Game. After all he had a lengthy list of things he wanted to buy and could always use more money. Although initially worried about all the stars Tom was earning,

Elaine and Roger realized that there was no cause for concern and no need to change anything, because Tom's behavior continued to improve and he liked the Game. Why tamper with success?

As a rule, if your child continues working hard to earn stars or check marks and enjoys turning them in for rewards or money, she is not earning too many, and you don't need to limit the number of check marks she can earn.

TAKING THE GAME ON THE ROAD

Once you feel you have some control at home, you can consider using the Game for those times when you and your child venture out of the house. Since many children have difficulty being good when they're out in public, here are some guidelines you can follow to help your child act better when you take him away from home, whether it's to the store, a restaurant, a friend's house, or anywhere else.

• **Before you leave home, prepare your child.**   Ahead of time, let your child know when and where you'll be going and how you want him to behave. The more you can prepare him by letting him know what you want him to do when you're out together, the better he will be.

• **Make up an "on the go," traveling Behavior Game.**   On an index card or something that's small and easy to carry around, make up a portable chart that lists the kinds of good behavior you want your child to demonstrate when she's out. Review this portable chart with her before you leave and be sure to take it with you.

• **Frequently praise your child for his good behavior.**   During your outing let your child know how pleased you are with his good behavior. Praise him for getting ready to go, and for acting nicely when you're out.

• **Put stars or check marks on your child's portable chart as she earns them**.   If you can, give your child the opportunity to cash in the stars or check marks she's earning while you're out. If this is impossible, make sure she gets to cash them in when you get home.

• **Offer a special reward if necessary.**   If it's very difficult for your child to do certain things when you're out in public (for example, if he's usually awful at the supermarket or he can't behave at a restaurant), you can offer him a special reward for being good during these difficult times.

• **If problem behavior occurs, follow through with your discipline plan.** If offering rewards for good behavior isn't enough and your child starts behaving badly, put your discipline plan into action. As you have for other problem behavior, make up a plan that combines warnings, ignoring, time-outs, the quiet chair, and taking away privileges or possessions. If your child is being truly impossible, you may need to come home and put her promptly into a time-out and perhaps take away a privilege for the rest of the day.

And remember, no matter where you're going or what you're doing, a portable, on-the-go, Behavior Game can help you out. So to encourage your child to behave himself and to prevent problems when you're out, don't leave home without your traveling Behavior Game. Before you know it, you'll be taking your child to museums, sporting events, amusement parks, and perhaps even on a vacation. Let's take a look at how a traveling Behavior Game can help your child behave when you're out shopping.

Going to the Store

Even the best-behaved child can turn into a monster at the store. We've all seen children grab boxes off the shelves or scream for candy. If your child has this problem, you're definitely not alone.

Let's take a look at some guidelines you can use to make going to the store less of a nightmare. Before you leave, remind your child of what you want him to do and of the reward he can earn for being good. Take along a portable chart that lists the different kinds of good behavior you want him to display; these might include getting ready to go to the store without a fuss, acting nicely in the car on the way, being good at the store by staying in the shopping cart or beside it, doing what is asked, being a good helper, talking nicely (no begging, crying, or whining) and, finally, behaving himself on the way home. You and your child may want to choose a small, inexpensive reward that he can buy with the stars he's earned for being good at the store.

If your child starts misbehaving at the store, ask her to stop and remind her of the stars she can earn for good behavior. If she keeps getting worse and ignoring doesn't work, you may need to leave the items you plan to buy temporarily and go to your car for a time-out so that she can settle down. When she's quieted down for a few minutes, you can return to the store and finish your shopping. Let's see how my client Elaine Markham used these guidelines to tame her daughter Susie when they went to the store.

Although the Behavior Game was helping Elaine's four-year-old daughter Susie at home, it hadn't made a dent in her behavior at the market. Elaine shared this all too familiar shopping nightmare with me. "Clean-up on aisle eleven." As the announcement came over the grocery-store speaker, Elaine was so embarrassed she wished she could disappear into the canned goods. She'd only turned her head for what seemed like a few seconds, but however long it was, it was plenty of time for her daughter Susie to drop and break several glass jars of tomato sauce. Now surrounded by thick red goo, they waited for the man with the mop. "Don't touch anything, there's glass everywhere," Elaine pleaded as Susie kneeled down to draw a face in the sauce. Why did Susie always cause such a ruckus? Why couldn't she and Susie go to the store like normal people, buy the items on their list, and then go home?

Working together Elaine and I made up a traveling Game for her to use with Susie at the market. As they were leaving to go shopping, Elaine would reward Susie for getting into the car without a fuss, listening to reminders about what she was supposed to do, and riding nicely to the store. Once at the store Susie could earn stars for staying by her mom, not touching anything on the shelves, and being good in the check-out line. As they shopped, Elaine would make sure to remind Susie that she could pick out a treat if she followed the "store rules." After only a week, Elaine was surprised at how quickly this on-the-go Game helped Susie when they went shopping. In fact, she confided in me that she had actually started looking forward to Susie's company when she went grocery shopping.

Visiting with Friends

If you avoid visiting with friends because your child is so unmanageable, invite your friends to your house first and let them see you use the Behavior Game while they're visiting. Let your child know that you want her to be your co-host, to be nice to your guests, to get along with their children, and to help out when asked. You can have her help you when you're preparing for your guests, when your company is visiting, and when you're cleaning up. You may want to let your child earn extra stars or check marks for helping out when friends are over.

Once your child is able to get along when friends visit you at your house, you can try using the Behavior Game when you visit friends at their houses. Always tell your child about your planned visit ahead of time so he has a time to get ready to go. Before you leave, review how you want him to act. Decide with your child on a reward he can earn for being good while visiting. After the visit is over, you may want to stop somewhere on the way home and get the reward or you may want to buy it ahead of time and give it to your child when your visit is over.

If your child acts up during your visit, put your discipline plan into action. Give your child a warning and ask her to stop. If she doesn't stop, either ignore her if you can or send her for a time-out or to a quiet chair. If your child continues to misbehave, and nothing is working, you may have to leave your friend's house. When you get home make sure your child gets a time-out. If your child is older, instead of using a time-out, you may want to take away a privilege such as seeing her friends for a day or two. Needless to say, don't give your child the reward she would have gotten for good behavior while visiting because she didn't earn it.

Let's see how my client Sophia Bernardo used these suggestions to help her son behave when they visited friends.

"You're bringing Jimmy? Are you sure that's a good idea?" Sophia knew why her friend Yvette was surprised that she wanted to include her five-year-old son when she visited. The last few times Jimmy had accompanied Sophia, he was unruly and impossible, fighting with the other children and throwing tantrums whenever he didn't get his way. But that was a month ago, before the Bernardos began playing the Behavior Game. Given the improvements Jimmy had made, Sophia was confident that she could avoid those problems by using a traveling Game during the visit. She prepped Jimmy by reviewing what she wanted him to do, and they decided on a reward of getting an inexpensive toy on the way home. Jimmy did a great job and bought an action toy he wanted. As they drove home Jimmy and Sophia talked about what fun they'd had on their visit.

Going Out to Eat

If you're like most parents, you have horror stories about taking your children out to eat. Before tackling this problem, make sure your child is earning stars or check marks for eating nicely at home. Once he's showing improvement at home, you can consider using the Behavior Game to help you when you go out to eat. When you go out it's a good idea to reward the same "eating nicely" behavior that you do at home. Choose a small reward to give your child if he's good. Perhaps he can get a pack of gum, a special dessert, or a small toy for his good behavior at mealtime.

If your child refuses to be good, give her a warning, and if this doesn't work, you can take her to the rest room or the car for a time-out. After she's quieted down, you can return to your meal and try again. If she just can't be good, you may need to go home and have a time-out at home. Younger children, especially when they're tired, may get so worked up that they just can't keep it together. If this happens, fill up your doggie bag and head home. You can always try again another day.

Ever since we began working together, my client Rosa Garcia would laugh when she talked about her fantasy of eating out in harmony with her daughters at a fast-food restaurant. Rosa could hardly contain herself when she told me about her first restaurant victory.

"For here or to go?" the cashier asked. Rosa smiled triumphantly as she said, "For here." She had prepped Lisa and Bonnie, seven and three, and was armed with a portable chart for each of them. She was confident that finally the family could eat out in peace. Rosa was right. Lisa and Bonnie were wonderful during the meal; Bonnie even cautioned her younger sister when she started whining for more catsup. Such exemplary behavior deserved a special reward. The girls got to pick out their favorite dessert. In fact, Rosa decided that on this special occasion she too should splurge and have dessert.

When you're ready to try your luck eating out, it's a good idea to start with an inexpensive restaurant that can quickly prepare food your child likes and where the staff is tolerant of young children. Stay away from fancy establishments that allow you to linger between courses and serve meals on fine china, at least when you're with your children.

INCLUDING OTHER ADULTS WHO CARE FOR YOUR CHILD

Once you feel comfortable playing the Game with your child, you can begin to extend it to other adults who take care of him. Here's how to get his other parent, baby-sitter, or teacher involved.

Involving Another Parent

If you've been playing the Behavior Game alone, but you and your child's other parent are together and living in the same household, it's likely that the uninvolved parent will come around in time just by watching the progress your child is making and by listening as your child extols the virtues of the Game. If you and your child's other parent are separated and your child visits him or her regularly, you'll probably need to take more direct action to get that parent involved. Whatever your situation, the following guidelines should help you as you recruit a new parent player:

• **Introduce the Game gradually.**   When talking about the Game to your child's other parent, don't go too fast. Even though the Game is "old hat" to you by now, remember it's still new to those who haven't had a chance to be involved in it yet.

Give the other person time to see the Game work. When others first hear about the Game, it's not unusual for them to be hesitant, ask a lot of questions, and develop a "wait-and-see" attitude. However, as they watch the Game work and your child improve, they'll usually warm up to it and want to get involved.

• **Have your child help sell the Game.**   Together with your child, talk about how the chart works and give examples of your child's kinds of good behavior and rewards. Most children are good salespeople and can bring even the most skeptical adult around.

• **Come up with a specific way for the other parent to participate.**   Because it's so important that everyone's first experience with the Game be positive, help the newly interested party pick an activity that he or she enjoys doing with your child, perhaps reading a story or playing a game. Have them do the activity together and then make sure your child gets a reward for his good behavior. As the other parent gets comfortable using rewards, introduce him or her to other components of the Game and offer to help develop a Good Behavior Chart and Reward Chart.

• **Always acknowledge the efforts of others who get involved.**   Use praise and encouragement with other adults who want to be included. And don't expect them to play exactly the same way that you do. Give them space to develop their own style. Give them time to learn how to reward correctly and use discipline techniques. Be available to offer support and guidance whenever needed but don't crowd them. Don't expect perfection.

Let's see how my client Rebecca Quentin put aside her differences with her ex-husband Carl when she and her son Matt talked to Carl about playing the Game.

After playing the Game for a few weeks, Matt, age seven, asked his mom Rebecca if she'd mind teaching his dad Carl how to play. Carl and Rebecca were divorced and Matt spent considerable time at his dad's house. Pleased that Matt wanted his dad to be involved, Rebecca asked me for advice on how to introduce Carl to the Game. Since Matt's enthusiasm about the Game was likely to be contagious, we decided that together both Rebecca and Matt should talk to Carl about the Game and how much Matt wanted to play when he visited. It turned out that this plan worked even better than we expected. No sooner had they started discussing the Game together, than Matt took over by explaining the Game to his dad and how much he liked it. Matt was so excited that Carl didn't bring up any objections and agreed to give it a try. Rebecca offered to help, but Matt and Carl assured her they could handle it. Although there were a few rough spots at the beginning, especially concerning when Matt would go to bed, in time things worked out and Matt and his dad played their version of the Game whenever Matt visited. Wisely, although it was difficult for her, Rebecca made sure not to intervene unless she was asked for help. I let Rebecca know how much I respected her for staying out of Matt's and his dad's Game and for putting Matt's need to have a good relationship with his father ahead of any negative feelings she might still have for Carl.

• **Recognize that your child's other parent may refuse to go along with the Game.**   Because there can be very strained relationships between parents, especially those who are separated and/or divorced, sometimes some parents won't play the Game as part of their general refusal to agree with anything their spouse or ex-spouse does. Or they may refuse to get involved because they don't believe in the techniques that the Game uses. For example, they may be opposed to rewarding children when they're good. When the other parent won't get involved, it's unfortunate but the Game can still work. It's not a good idea to get into a power struggle over the Game. Trying to force someone to play tends to make the Game negative for your child. So, if your child's other parent refuses to play, accept his or her refusal and do the best you can on your own.

• **In spite of any resistance you meet, hang in there.**   Try ignoring any negative comments people may make about the Game. If this doesn't work, you can change the subject and not discuss the Game with them. And if necessary, let them know that in spite of their objections, you're going to keep playing the Game.

Getting Your Baby-Sitter to Participate

If your child spends a lot of time with a baby-sitter, it's a good idea to get her involved in the Game. Usually caregivers are enthusiastic about the Game because it helps them keep their charges under control. So when you're ready, here are some guidelines to help you bring your child's baby-sitter onboard.

• **Explain the Game and ask for your baby-sitter's help.**   With your child by your side, show your sitter the chart you've been using and have your child tell her about the rewards he's been earning. Let her know how much better the Game will work if she'll help you out and join in.

• **Make up a special chart for her to use.**   With your baby-sitter's input, make up a list of the kinds of good behavior she'd like to see your child display, such as getting along, doing what is asked, helping out, and doing homework.

• **Decide what to do about rewards.**   Although your child will be earning stars or check marks from the sitter, he may or may not get to cash them in with her. However, if it's feasible for your child to buy rewards while he's with the baby-sitter, then you and your baby-sitter need to choose his rewards and how they will be earned. It's best to adopt a plan similar to the one you use regularly at home. For example, your baby-sitter can offer your child the chance to buy fifteen minutes of free time or a treat when your child has earned enough stars or check marks.

If your baby-sitter is reluctant to offer rewards, you can have your child wait to spend her stars or check marks until she gets home. If there are a number of children at your child's day-care location, your baby-sitter may find it difficult to allow only your child to buy rewards when the other children aren't able to. In this situation, it may be better for your child to wait until she gets home to spend her stars or check marks. If you use this delayed-reward system, it's a good idea to make a note card listing the kinds of good behavior you both want to see for each day. Have the baby-sitter put down the stars or check marks earned and have your child bring the card home. Use the card to determine what rewards your child can buy.

• **Be available when needed.**   Make sure your baby-sitter feels free to call you if she has a question or if your child is giving her a hard time. When you pick up your child you can get a progress report and offer words of support, encouragement, and reassurance.

• **Make it a united effort and be patient.**   Don't expect perfection. Remember, it will take your baby-sitter some time to get the knack of the Game. To help her learn how to play the Game you may want to have the baby-sitter watch you and your child as you use the chart and reward good behavior. You can also try to be there for a little while on the first day when she tries out the chart to offer any necessary help.

• **If needed, involve your baby-sitter in your discipline plan.**   If your baby-sitter has been using the Game for a few weeks, but continues having problems getting some of your child's behavior under control, you can share your discipline plan with her.

Depending on the particular problems your child is having with the baby-sitter, develop a plan that includes warnings, ignoring, time-out and/or taking away possessions or privileges for a short time. For example, if you're using a warning and then time-out for rough play, have her do the same. If you're using a warning, ignoring, and time-out for begging and whining, again, have her do that as well. Make sure to review carefully how to use each of the techniques, especially time-out or the quiet chair. Talk about specific situations and what you think are the best things to try.

If your baby-sitter is reluctant to use your discipline plan, don't force her to. Just make sure she is willing to use the chart and provide your child with stars or check marks. And of course, never allow your baby-sitter to use physical punishment of any kind.

And as a final note, if your sitter won't go along with the positive side of the Game, I find it's usually best to cut your losses and spend some time looking for another baby-sitter. Although this may sound harsh, when you think about it, the last thing your child needs is a baby-sitter who doesn't believe in praise and encouragement.

Let's see how my client Brad Pitzer used these tips to get his daughter's baby-sitter involved:

Nothing had prepared Brad Pitzer for being a single dad. Trying to be there for his six-year-old daughter Julie while holding down a demanding job was overwhelming at times, especially since her behavior had become so difficult to deal with. When Brad came to see me and discovered the Behavior Game he felt as though he had gained a much-needed friend. After he was comfortable playing the Game with Julie, he wanted to include her baby-sitter, Maryanne, as well. But like many parents I work with he was hesitant to talk to Maryanne about the Game. What if she didn't like the idea of rewarding Julie and using a chart? What would he do then? Fortunately, it turned out that Brad had nothing to worry about. Julie had already spilled the beans and told Maryanne all about how great the Game was. So when Brad brought it up, Maryanne was raring to go. Together all three made up a chart that Maryanne could use with Julie. Thinking back, Brad wondered what he'd been so worried about. As we continued working together, he became more hopeful that being a single father wasn't going to be as impossible as he had feared.

Bringing Your Child's Teacher Onboard

The Behavior Game can usually help children do better in school. By using the Game at home and rewarding your child for bringing his schoolwork home, doing homework for short periods of time, and taking his work back to school, you may have already seen improvement in your child's school behavior. Often, the home Game is enough and your child doesn't need anything more. Since most teachers are overloaded and find it difficult to use an individual chart for one student, as a rule you should not ask for your child's teacher to help you unless you feel that you must. However, if your child is having difficulty behaving in class, his teacher may welcome the idea of a good behavior chart and rewards. If you do decide you want to include your child's teacher, here are some suggestions to follow:

•   **Arrange for a teacher conference.**   Explain to your child's teacher that you've been playing the Behavior Game, why you've been playing it, and how it works. You and your child's teacher may discover that the Behavior Game is very similar to some of the classroom systems she uses to encourage academic performance and to reward good behavior. If she seems interested, together you can develop a chart for her to use with your child in the classroom.

•   **Create a classroom chart.**   Discuss your child's problem and good behaviors in the classroom. Together, come up with a list of kinds of good behavior that both of you would like to see your child develop and list them on a small, easy-to-carry card, perhaps a 3-x-5-inch index card. This behavior may include listening when the teacher talks, not interrupting, paying attention, doing schoolwork when asked, getting along with other children, not fighting, not teasing, not name-calling, and playing nicely on the playground.

•   **Decide how the chart will work.**   Most parents I work with use a system in which the teacher makes a check beside each kind of good behavior on the chart when the child behaves well, is showing improvement, or at least is trying. At the end of each day the teacher initials the chart and has the child take it home. If he wants to add any comments, he can do this at the bottom of the card. Your child brings his chart home every day so that you can see how he's doing and provide him with an at-home reward for his efforts.

•   **Help your child's teacher.**   Since your child's teacher is likely to be very busy, offer to make your child's daily classroom chart and supply copies to the teacher perhaps a week at a time. When you make your child's daily chart include his name, the date, and the kinds of good behavior that you and your child's teacher developed. Provide a space beside each kind of behavior for check marks, a space for the teacher's initials, and room for comments.

•   **Keep track of how your child is doing.**   When your child brings home his chart, you can let him know how pleased you are with his progress and help him transfer the checks he earned in school onto his game at home. Just as he does with other check marks or stars, your child can use these to buy rewards from his Reward Chart.

•   **Check in regularly with your child's teacher.**   Keep in touch with your child's teacher to make sure that she feels the chart is working. As your child improves, you and her teacher may want to change the kinds of behavior listed on her chart and make them a little harder to perform. Always let her teacher know how much you appreciate her help. After a while, your child may not need a classroom chart anymore.

If your child continues to have problems at school, he may need more than a classroom Game. When this situation occurs, ask your child's teacher for his advice, check with the school psychologist or counselor, and talk about what can be done to help your child. You may want to check with your child's doctor as well.

• **Don't force your child's teacher to participate in the Game.**   It rarely works to try to force a teacher to get involved. If your child's teacher doesn't want to play, it's probably because she doesn't have the time to devote to a special chart for your child.

This was the situation when my clients Hector and Teresa Ruiz talked to their daughter's teacher about the Game.

Hector and Teresa Ruiz were so excited about the Game that they wanted everyone involved with their seven-year-old daughter Rachel to participate. So when it was time for their fall teacher conference, they mentioned to Rachel's teacher that she enjoyed playing the Behavior Game at home and that they'd seen a lot of good changes. Although her teacher felt that it was great that Rachel was involved in a reward system, she was lukewarm about the idea of using the Game at school. After she explained that she didn't have the time to fill out a chart just for Rachel every day, Rachel's teacher shared the classroom incentive system she used for all her students. Hector and Teresa were pleasantly surprised with how similar it was to the Behavior Game that Rachel was playing at home.

Encouraging Tutors and Coaches to Get Involved

If needed, you may want to include other adults such as tutors, coaches, or instructors who work with your child. You can use the same ideas suggested for teachers to help your child behave better when he's participating in extra-curricular activities, whether tutoring sessions, music lessons, religion classes, or sports practice. If your child is having difficulties in an activity, find out from his instructor or coach what the problems are and what your child should be doing. Let the instructor know that you'll be working with your child to help him improve. Ask your child's instructor to watch carefully for improvement and let you know how your child did after each lesson.

Include improving behavior at this activity as part of your child's chart. Talk with your child about what you're adding to the Game and be sure to remind her before the activity about how you'd like her to behave. When the activity is over, ask her teacher, coach, or instructor how she did. If the report is good, make sure she earns stars or check marks or gets a treat for her efforts.

In some cases a child may need his instructor or tutor to use a portable chart and award stars and check marks. If this is the case with your child, work closely with your child's tutor or instructor and together make a chart he can use.

For further information on the topics covered in this chapter, you can refer to the references listed in Appendix B.

Now that you've learned how to raise standards for your child's behavior gradually, how to take the Game on the road, and how to get other adult caregivers involved, let's take a look at how you can use the Game as a foundation in building better communication with your child.

7

COMMUNICATING WITH YOUR CHILD

In previous chapters you've focused directly on behavior and how to get it to change. If the Game has gone well, your child should be behaving better. If you've been able to lay this foundation of good behavior, you're ready to tackle the stormy weather of parent-child communication.

Kids drive their parents crazy when they won't talk with them, and even when they do talk, they constantly complain about their lot in life. Creating a family environment that fosters free and open give-and-take is always difficult. Every family struggles to communicate. This chapter will give you some ideas about how to talk and listen to your child. It will also describe how to help her to see the bright side and how to solve her own problems.

I recommend that you feel positive about your child and the improvements he's made before you begin this chapter. So if necessary, spend a few more weeks using the Game before beginning your efforts at improving communication. This process is always easier if your child is receptive to your comments. If your child has been playing the Behavior Game, he should be more open to your ideas and more willing to listen. So when you think that everyone is ready, give the following guidelines a try. Please remember, this chapter is intended only as an introduction to the concept of communication—there are whole books written on the subject.

LISTENING AND TALKING TO YOUR CHILD

The guidelines below will provide you with a starting point as you focus your efforts on encouraging your child to listen and talk to you:

- **Set aside a time every day to talk to your child.** A good time to do this is during one or more of the discussion times you have already set up. Whether it's after school, when you get home from work, in the evening, and/ or before bedtime, encourage your child to talk to you.
- **During discussion time invite your child to talk to you.** Let your child know you're looking forward to talking with her and that you're interested in what she has to say. In fact, if possible, whenever your child wants to talk try to spend a few minutes listening. This is especially important if your child tends to be the quieter type and is hesitant to talk.

Don't push your child if he doesn't want to say much about his day. It's okay if your child doesn't feel like talking during discussion time. Let him know that you'd like to listen when he's ready to talk to you. Spend the time doing something together and try asking him again later whether he wants to talk. Some children are practically gushing with information when they get home from school, while others only drop hints throughout the afternoon and evening. Still others wait until it's bedtime to talk about their day. If this is when your child usually wants to talk to you, make sure you start talking early enough so that your child can get to bed on time.

Most of my clients have worked this time into their Behavior Games just as my client Allison Patil did.

Her six-year-old daughter Betsy was so quiet during discussion time that Allison decided to play Betsy's favorite game, Go Fish, as an icebreaker. As they drew and discarded, Allison talked a little about her own day and then casually asked Betsy what happened to her at school, with her friends or at recess. Since communicating was difficult for Betsy, Allison made sure to reward her with stars on her chart for spending time listening and talking with her mother. As Betsy got used to this "talking time" as she called it, she became more comfortable opening up about what was going on.

- **Listen carefully.** When your child is talking, listen carefully. Make sure your child knows you are listening to her. Look at her, smile when appropriate, and nod. Whenever possible give her your full attention. If you get interrupted, make sure to continue your conversation as soon as you can.
- **Don't interrupt.** Be quiet when your child is talking to you. Wait to speak until your child is finished with what he is saying. Don't make a com-

ment or ask a question until he's completed his thought. If he stops and you're not sure whether he's finished, ask him.

•   **Show interest by making supportive comments or asking questions.** When your child is finished talking let her know that you appreciated her sharing her experiences with you. If she's telling you about something she learned at school you might say something such as, "That was interesting," and then encourage her to tell you more. For example, if your child is telling you about a difficult test she took, you could show support by saying something like, "It sounds as if you thought it was a tough test. What were some of the questions?" However, don't ask your child questions that challenge what she is saying. For example, don't ask her, "What do you mean you think it was hard? Didn't you study enough?" If your child feels as if you're putting her on the spot, it will discourage her from talking to you. Don't press your child or drill her for every detail.

•   **Encourage your child to listen and not interrupt when you or others speak.**   Help your child learn the importance of listening carefully and not interrupting. Remind him when you want him to listen and make sure to let him know when he's doing a good job. If he interrupts you, ask him to wait until you're finished. When you're done talking, thank him for listening and ask him what he wanted to say. If he tends to interrupt his siblings, suggest that he listen until they are finished and then take his turn. If he still interrupts, ask him to stop and let his sibling finish speaking.

Coping with Complaints

An important part of communicating is complaining. Everyone likes the chance to complain and be heard. Your child is no exception. Even if your child tends to be happy-go-lucky, he still needs the opportunity to vent his feelings about his day, especially as he gets older. Your child needs an atmosphere in which he feels comfortable telling you about what's going wrong. By using the techniques described below, you'll be able to handle your child's complaining in a productive fashion:

•   **Just listen and don't try to fix things.**   When your child is talking about what isn't going right, it may not be necessary or possible or even advisable to do anything more than listen and then tell your child that you care. That may be all your child needs or can handle for now. Sometimes children just want to let off steam and have a friendly, caring person listen to them. They don't always want to talk at length about what upsets them, and they don't necessarily want to try to change anything. So no matter how hard it is, keep your mouth shut and let your child talk.

Let's see how my client Joel used these ideas to cope with his son's complaints:

"It hurts to hear my child talk about things that went wrong. I can't stand just sitting there," Joel told me. On a recent afternoon he found it particularly difficult to listen when his five-year-old son George came home with tales about how all the kids made fun of him because he didn't climb to the top of the jungle gym. Although he wanted to chime in and tell George how to fight back and make all the other kids leave him alone, Joel took my advice and just listened instead. As George continued his story it became clear that only one boy had made fun of him and that the children weren't supposed to climb to the top without an adult supervising. By biting his tongue, Joel had given George a chance to tell the whole story. Of equal importance, by letting George talk, his dad was encouraging him to share his feelings.

• **If your child goes on and on, you may want to set a time limit**.   No matter how understanding you want to be, you'll be able to listen to your child complain for only so long. Set a time limit and then interrupt with a supportive statement and change the subject. For example, if every day your child goes on and on about how awful school was, you may decide to listen for five minutes, then let your child know you're sorry her day didn't go well and change the subject. In the next section of this chapter we'll take a look at some ways you can change the subject and switch to a focus on positive experiences.

• **Let your child know how upset you'd feel if the same thing happened to you**.   After your child is finished complaining, you may want to let him know that you would feel pretty bad if your day had gone like his. Children need reassurance that everyone has frustrations and disappointments, especially their parents. It's also important to remind your child that no matter how hard he tries there will still be bad days when nothing seems to go right.

• **Encourage your child to forget about "stupid, unavoidable little things" that happen.**   Everyone does embarrassing things like spilling milk at lunch, missing an easy catch, or tripping in front of everyone during gym class. Trying to forget is usually a good idea for things that aren't very important, couldn't be helped, or that hardly ever happen. Also, you may want to encourage your child not to dwell on situations that convince her that "life is unfair."

Sometimes you can put unpleasant situations into perspective by using humor. For example, in my family we try to find something funny about an embarrassing situation. Life would be a lot tougher if we didn't try to laugh about the absurdity of it. When my children are down in the dumps about an embarrassing situation or a mistake they made, I try to come up with one of the many faux pas from my past. Here's one of their favorite stories: As an eighth grader at my first formal dance, I was dancing with a ninth-grade boy I had a crush on. I was so excited. This was heaven. Unfortunately paradise was fleeting. A brief glance downward was all it took to destroy the mood. My crinoline slip had fallen and was standing up around my feet. I had no choice but to step out of it, take it to the ladies room, and abandon it. The dance ended, nothing came of my big crush, and no matter how often I dressed up after that, I never wore the slip again.

If humor works in your family, use it. Being able to laugh about one's mistakes and go on is an invaluable skill that will serve you and your child well, now and in the future. It's important to strike the right balance. Never make fun of your child, but whenever possible try to find the humor in even the worst situations. And if your experiences have been anything like mine, you'll discover that you have plenty of amusing and illustrative experiences to share with your child.

Putting a Positive Spin on Your Child's Day

Although almost all children have complaining down pat, some are not nearly as skilled when it comes to reporting the good things that happen to them. It's important that your child acknowledge the positive things in his life. By paying attention to things that went well and to his efforts and accomplishments, your child will strengthen his self-esteem and sense of self-worth. As a rule, so long as your child is realistic, the more your child believes in himself, the better off he will be. Here are some ways you can make sure your child doesn't miss the good things that happen to him:

- **Review your child's day and point out what went well.** Ask your child to tell you about her day, pick out those things you feel were good, identify them for your child, and tell her why you think they're good. Don't worry if your child doesn't agree with you and insists that nothing good happened. In time, your upbeat interpretations can help your child see things in a more positive light.

- **Using a scale of one to ten, help your child rate events in his day.** While this may sound contrived, your child may enjoy it. By rating events your child can learn to differentiate along a continuum from very bad, a one rating, to very good, a ten rating. As you and your child rate events you'll probably find that the ends of the continuum are usually easy to agree on, getting an "A" or kicking a goal are clearly tens; while failing a test or going to the principal's office are obviously ones. However, most experiences fall in between. Improving in math, finishing a project, or getting picked for a team may be on the upper end of the continuum, while missing a question in class, forgetting to turn in an assignment, or not being invited to a party may be on the lower end of the scale. Don't worry if your child isn't sure about a rating or if he rates an event differently from the way you would. The important part is to spend time talking about these events and putting them into perspective.

- **Encourage your child to come up on his own with something good that happened.** Some children respond well to being challenged to come up with something they did well. With practice your child should continue getting better at differentiating between the bad and the good and eventually be able to report the good things on his own without your assistance.

Let's see how my client Mark Adams used these techniques with his son Ryan:

Mark and I agreed that he would need all these techniques if he was going to help his ten-year-old son Ryan improve his outlook on life. Mark told me that every evening Ryan, alias Mr. Doom-and-Gloom, held forth about how nothing ever went right at school. Everyone and everything was "unfair." Although Mark wanted to chime in immediately and point out how negative Ryan was being, we agreed that he needed to bite his tongue and give Ryan a chance to let off some steam. After Ryan had a chance to rant and rave, Mark could change the focus and point out things that had gone well for

Ryan during the day. After doing this for several days, Mark and I agreed that he should try introducing Ryan to the idea of a rating scale.

The next week when I saw Mark, he couldn't wait to tell me about how Ryan had responded to rating his day. According to Mark, from the start Ryan was intrigued by the idea of using a rating scale and took great delight in assigning a numerical value to all the awful things that had happened to him. But as Ryan evaluated each situation, he discovered that some were not as horrible as others. For example, Ryan had to admit that only missing two out of twenty spelling words was not as much of a disaster as being picked tenth for kick ball at recess. Instead of concentrating only on what he had done wrong during the first week, Ryan began to recognize that he also did some things well. He had to admit that he was a pretty good soccer player and enjoyed playing forward on his team. Hearing this made Mark happy, for although he had no desire for Ryan to see the world through rose-colored glasses, Mark hoped that eventually Ryan would be able to appreciate and enjoy some good times.

I hope that your child, like Ryan, will be able to benefit from some of the techniques you just read about. And as you and your child become more comfortable about sharing experiences, you may want to begin engaging your child in the problem-solving process.

HELPING YOUR CHILD SOLVE PROBLEMS

Growing up can seem like a never-ending series of problems—family problems, friendship problems, and school problems, to name just a few. Problems are a normal, unavoidable part of life so no matter how good a parent you are or how fabulous your child is, there are bound to be problems.

Learning to acknowledge one's own problems and then taking steps to solve them is an ongoing, complicated trial-and-error process. Here are some ways that you can introduce the problem-solving process to your child:

•   **Work together.**   Make sure your child is actively involved in solving her problems. Avoid the temptation to solve them for her. Even though you may have a good idea of what the problem is and how it can be improved, work together with your child to define the problem and come up with a solution. No matter how much extra time it takes, include your child in the process.

• **Go slowly.**   Most problems take a lot of time, effort, and patience to solve. Solutions can't be rushed, and you and your child need to feel ready to tackle a problem before beginning this usually difficult task. Your child needs to take his time and go step-by-step. So try to relax and don't offer your opinion unless the problem is a serious, harmful, or dangerous situation that demands immediate action.

• **Stop the process whenever you or your child wants to.**   Don't expect your child to finish solving a problem in one sitting. It may take several days, perhaps even weeks, to come up with a plan. So don't worry if, after talking with you for a while, your child decides she doesn't want to do anything about the problem. This is not uncommon. For many reasons your child may decide she's not ready to tackle a problem. But you haven't wasted your time. Talking with your child about a problem helps her become aware of it and makes it easier to solve in the future.

Let's see how this perspective helped my client Sherry MacDonald understand that her daughter Gina was making progress with problem solving.

Although they were getting along much better, Sherry was frustrated because her eleven-year-old daughter Gina couldn't seem to make any progress when it came to solving problems with friends. Sherry confided in me that Gina always gave up before they finished solving the problem. For example, only the day before, after Sherry and Gina had spent at least fifteen minutes talking about how Gina could apologize and patch things up with her best friend Kelly, Gina announced that she didn't want to talk about it anymore. All the work they had done seemed like a waste of time.

I encouraged Sherry to be patient because even though she was frustrated, Gina was making some progress. I pointed out that at least Gina had begun to think about different things she could try and perhaps soon she'd be ready to put one of her ideas into action. As a matter of fact, during the next week, Gina shared her ideas about how to win Kelly back with Sherry. Gina wanted to invite Kelly over as soon as possible. She was sure they would have a great time listening to music and watching their favorite television show. As it turned out, Gina was right, Gina and Kelly got along famously and had a great time. Their friendship had weathered another storm.

Spend Time Talking with Your Child about What's Upsetting Her

Before a problem can be solved, it needs to be clearly defined. Figuring out what is bothering your child is usually harder than you think it will be. Different children experience problems differently. Sometimes children are upset but don't know why. If this happens to your child, help him figure out what events upset him. Have him review his day and think about the different things that happened and how they made him feel. If he's having difficulty doing this, as you slowly review his day, you can ask him leading questions such as, "What happened when you got to school, . . . in class, . . . at recess, . . . at lunch, . . . with your friends?" If a particular situation seems to have upset him, you can ask him more about it. Try to ask gentle nonaccusatory follow-up questions: "What happened at recess that upset you?" "When your friend was teasing you, how did that feel?"

If your child is like most children, she will blame others for her problems. Don't be surprised if your child denies responsibility and pleads "not guilty" on all counts. For example, if she's having a problem at school she may feel it's because she has an unfair teacher who gives too much homework, or if she's having arguments with her best friend, it's likely to be her friend's fault. If your child places blame, help her refocus and think about what she does in the situation.

Help Your Child Describe How He Acts When the Problem Happens

Like the other steps in problem solving, this one is rarely easy. Your child is likely to be adamant that other people, not him, need to change their behavior and make the problem go away. This is certainly understandable. If given the choice, who wouldn't like others to change and behave differently? Unfortunately, wishing doesn't make things happen. The bottom line is that if your child wants something to change, he'll need to take action himself. If he waits for others to come around, he's likely to be in for a long, unproductive wait.

As you work through the problem-solving process, instead of concentrating on whose fault a problem is or insisting that your child take responsibility for the problem, try coming at it from a different direction. Encourage your child to talk about what he did when the problem occurred. Initially this may be especially difficult for your child because he hasn't thought about his part in the problem or won't want to talk about it. Your child may tell you that he did "nothing," or it may take him a long time to remember what he did. Again, don't push him. Give him time to think about it. Once you have an idea about what your child is doing, you can switch gears and begin talking about different ways he could behave in similar situations.

Come Up with a Plan of Action

What you and your child decide to do will depend on the particular problem, how bad it is, and what steps your child feels comfortable taking. If the problem rarely occurs, you may decide it's not worth doing anything about. If a problem demands your attention, the strategy your child tries should be based on what she does well. For example, although being teased is a common problem, the solution your child chooses should depend on what your child feels comfortable with. If your child is outgoing and assertive, she may choose to tell her peers directly to leave her alone; on the other hand, if your child is shy and quiet, she may feel better ignoring her classmates and walking away.

Always start off by listening, offering support and sharing similar experiences. But when that isn't enough, here are some action plans you can consider. As you read through the following strategies, keep your own child's strengths in mind and help her choose those techniques that you think would work best for her. And remember, even though these solutions sound rational and straightforward, they're rarely easy for your child to carry out in the heat of the situation.

• **Do nothing at all.**   Sometimes after analyzing a problem you and your child may decide that the best course of action is to take no action and to try to forget about what happened. This approach usually works well for infrequent problems that happen to everyone. For example, sooner or later every child feels rejection, whether it's because he wasn't invited to a party or she wasn't picked for a team. After your child has told you about the situation and you've talked about how bad being left out can feel, it's usually a good idea to change your focus and talk about other things. Dwelling on the unpleasant event only makes everyone feel worse.

• **Give the problem some time.**   Rather than rush into a solution, you and your child may decide to wait to see whether things get better in a day or two. Although it can be difficult to wait, sometimes it's the best approach. After a good night's sleep what seemed like a huge problem may seem much more manageable. When your child argues with a friend over little issues like who goes first or the rules of a game, some time away from each other can be just what the doctor ordered. While tempers can flare up quickly, they usually die down quickly as well. In a day or two your child will forget about the fight and be ready to play with his friend again.

• **Try being better prepared.**   Practicing ahead of time can be beneficial in preventing a problem from happening again, especially in the classroom. While this idea may seem obvious to parents, many children find it difficult to grasp. A child usually needs a number of trials before he learns that his preparation and effort can favorably affect outcome. Here are a few examples of how you can encourage your child to practice and improve. If your child goes over his spelling words several times and can spell them at home, he's likely to do better on his spelling test. If he practices his addition tables, he'll probably get better at doing them. If your child gets nervous and misses questions in class, try rehearsing the situation in a relaxed atmosphere. Between the two of you, alternate the parts of teacher and student. Ask him questions and then have him ask you questions. This practice will help him recognize the link between preparation and improvement.

• **Ignore, leave, or avoid unchangeable situations.**   Sometimes even though your child wants to do something to change a situation, realistically there's almost nothing she can do. If at recess other children delight in teasing your child, her best choice may be to ignore it. Sometimes children will quit teasing if they get no response. If this doesn't work she can leave the group of children who are bothering her and find other children to play with. She may want to avoid the teasers in the future.

• **Cool off.**   Since all children get angry from time to time, it's a good idea for your child to learn how to calm down and stay in control. For most children, losing control feels scary and upsetting. Although it's impossible to stay calm at all times, there are some things your child can try. He can count to ten, walk away, or ignore what's going on and do something else. When helping your child plan his strategy, you may also find it helpful to spend some time talking about what your child would *like* to do compared to what he *should* do. Your child may want to slug his friend or call his teacher an "unfair, stupid jerk"; however, instead, he should try to walk away from his friend and "bite his tongue" in front of the teacher. Let your child know that sometimes even you, his parent, feel like you're going to lose control, and then share the kinds of things you do to behave the way you should.

•   **Apologize and patch things up.**   When your child has a fight with a friend, encourage her to spend some time cooling off and talking about what happened. Suggest that your child "sleep on" the problem and see how she feels about it in the morning. If your child is still upset about what happened, you may want to help her practice how to talk to her friend about the problem. You can pretend to be her friend and have her practice talking to you. When she's ready, she may want to talk to her friend and try to solve the problem they're having. As your child gets older, encourage her to try to solve problems with friends on her own. Older children are usually able to do a pretty good job of patching things up. Learning to apologize can go a long way toward preserving friendships. So although it may be difficult for your child, help her find some "graceful" ways to apologize.

In hopes that all of these ideas haven't confused you too much but rather alerted you to the never-ending challenge of problem solving, let's look in on the Bradleys as they use the techniques you just read about to rescue Cindy from what she believes to be the permanent loss of her best friend, Ellen.

Cindy burst into the living room in tears. "Nobody likes me," she sobbed.

"What happened?" Joan asked.

"Ellen said she's never going to play with me again! She said she hates me!"

As he put his arm around her, Gary suggested, "Let's talk about what happened."

Cindy began by talking about how they had been playing school that afternoon. Cindy was busy being the teacher and Ellen was the student and everything was going just fine until Ellen, all of a sudden, decided that she wanted to be the teacher. Cindy didn't want to change and be the student. She wanted to keep being the teacher. Ellen got mad and told Cindy to go home and that she never wanted to play with her again. So Cindy came home, and here she was without a friend in the world. She was convinced that she had just lost her best friend forever.

Listening intently, Joan and Gary made sure not to interrupt while Cindy told her story. When Cindy was finished, Joan started talking to her about what had happened. Joan was especially interested in how Ellen and Cindy usually played school. Cindy told Joan that she was usually the teacher and

Ellen was usually the student, and that this never bothered Ellen. And anyway, Cindy liked being teacher best and frankly thought she did a better job of it than Ellen did.

Gary asked Cindy to think about other ways they might play school together. Together, they talked about sharing and taking turns and how maybe, even though Cindy might be better at playing teacher, she should give Ellen a chance to be teacher from time to time. Finally, Gary asked Cindy what she wanted to do about the problem she was having with Ellen.

"It doesn't matter what I do! It's too late! Ellen hates me," Cindy said.

"Maybe not. Why not call Ellen after dinner, tell her you're sorry about the fight you had, and ask her if she'd like to come here to play tomorrow and see if she'd like to be teacher."

When Cindy called Ellen, she found that Ellen wanted to play after all.

Most of Cindy's problems won't be solved so easily and neither will your child's. But you'll never know unless you try. By following the guidelines I've suggested you'll encourage your child to begin tackling her own problems. And to motivate your child to continue this often frustrating process, be sure to add her problem-solving efforts to her Behavior Game chart.

Once again, this chapter was intended as only an introduction to the art of communication and problem solving. For further information you can refer to the books listed in Appendix B.

You've seen incredible progress. The Behavior Game has given you a fun way to increase your child's good behavior and reduce his discipline problems. It's provided a mechanism for raising your behavior standards and improving communication and problem-solving skills. Weeks of working at and playing the Game have paid off.

It's time to take stock and look ahead. Part Three, chapters 8 and 9, explains how to evaluate your Game and keep it fresh and vital for the many months and years it can continue to help your family.

PART THREE

PERPETUATING A GOOD THING

Keeping the Game Going
and Up-to-Date

8

KEEPING THE GAME GOING

In this chapter I'll discuss how to review the changes your child has made and decide whether you need additional help with problems the Game hasn't helped you solve. After that, we'll look ahead to playing the Game in the future, and then pause for a moment to celebrate your victories so far.

REVIEWING CHANGES YOUR CHILD HAS MADE

After you've successfully played the Game for six to eight weeks, it's time to take stock of how far you've come. Ask yourself each of the questions that follow. As you're answering, keep in mind that some of the behavior changes described may take a long time to occur. So if they haven't happened for your child yet, don't be discouraged. You may have to give the Game more time.

• **Has your child's behavior improved?** Since it's easy to forget what your child's behavior was like before you began playing the Game, you may want to remind yourself about how things were by taking a look at the Good Behavior Checklist you filled out earlier. As you look at this checklist notice how you originally rated each kind of behavior (often, sometimes, rarely, never) and then think about how you would rate that same behavior today. Is your child acting the way you want more often?

Let's see what happened when my clients, Beth and Dave Williams, compared their son Dan's behavior as it was originally and how it had changed since they began playing the Game.

151

As Beth and Dave Williams looked over their seven-year-old son Dan's Good Behavior Checklist, they couldn't help but smile. In the past six weeks Dan had improved on all fronts, most notably in his attitude toward his parents. Before Beth and Dave began the Game, if they asked Dan to help with the dishes or straighten up his room, he ignored them or promised to do it later. Occasionally, if they kept begging him, he'd make a halfhearted attempt by taking his plate and glass to the sink and then make a beeline for the television. Fortunately the prospect of earning rewards changed Dan's approach to helping out. With check marks on the line, he usually did what his parents asked and sometimes even volunteered to help.

Beth, Dave, and I talked about how important it was that they had quit nagging Dan about everything they wanted him to do and instead supplied him with incentives to help them. With this change, Dan no longer experienced his parents as negative and badgering. Instead he saw them as the bearers of good news—the source of positive comments and rewards. Instead of avoiding Beth and Dave, Dan started to seek them out.

• **Is your child sharing more with you?** By encouraging your child to talk and listen, she should be opening up and confiding in you more often. Think about recent discussion times you've spent with your child. Are the two of you able to talk about her positive and negative feelings and experiences?

Let's see how my clients the Browns used their share time to encourage their daughter Meg to talk to them.

Five-year-old Meg, the ever-silent one, was finally opening up to her parents, Chris and Kelly. Since they stopped interrogating her every day about what happened at kindergarten and began to listen to her instead, Meg began to tell them what had happened at school. One time recently, Meg had shared her excitement about Julie, a new friend, and what fun they'd had cutting and pasting pictures of their pets in scrapbooks they were making. When Meg asked her mom if she could have Julie over soon, Kelly was quick to say, "Of course." Chris and Kelly were very pleased that they were beginning to communicate with Meg and that she seemed to enjoy rattling on about recess or reading period or other daily activities.

Chris, Kelly, and I talked about how this change in Meg had come about largely because they had stopped interrupting her, pestering her, and criticizing her, and started showing their concern instead, waiting until she felt like talking and providing a friendly ear. This environment was just what Meg needed to open up and begin sharing her experiences with her parents.

• **Is your family getting along better?** Think about how your family interacted before the Game and compare that to what it's like when you're together now. Are there fewer arguments and fights? Does your family do more together than they used to?

Let's see how playing the Game helped my clients the Scotts start doing things together again.

"A family picnic? You've got to be kidding." Mary Scott's grandmother Edith wasn't used to going on family gatherings with her five-year-old grand-daughter. Mary behaved so badly that her parents, Jim and Midge, had stopped trying to do anything as a family. For months, they'd made excuses to Edith about why they couldn't plan anything. But several weeks into the Game, they felt confident enough to try a picnic and invited Edith along. By using a portable chart, Jim and Midge helped Mary show everyone at the picnic, especially her Grandma Edith, what a good girl she could be. Although skeptical at first, after several more outings, Grandma Edith had to admit that Mary's improvement wasn't a fluke. Her good behavior was real all right. Edith even asked to have Mary visit her alone without her parents, provided of course that Midge and Jim make up a Behavior Game chart for Edith to use with Mary.

• **Is your child trying harder?** By encouraging small steps of progress, you should be helping your child put forth additional effort. Because your support makes your child feel like he can succeed, he isn't as likely to give up. Watch your child when he's doing his schoolwork or when he's tackling a chore and see how long he's able to stick with it. Is he doing better than he did before you started playing the Game? Is he able to concentrate on his homework? Is he trying at school?

Let's see how rewarding short amounts of time helped my clients the Webbs encourage their daughter to do her school assignments.

Peggy Webb, age ten, always started her homework with a burst of enthusiasm. But after a few minutes, she'd fizzle out, become distracted, and start daydreaming. Nagging her didn't help, neither did long lectures on why she should do her homework. However, once her parents, Natalie and Trevor, started rewarding Peggy for short study periods, she got much better about settling down and doing her assignments. As Peggy explained to her parents, even though the work was sometimes hard, she liked getting her work done and getting a reward for doing it.

When Natalie, Trevor, and I talked about Peggy's improvement, they were especially surprised with Peggy's pride in completing her work. Peggy almost glowed with satisfaction, her father Trevor reported. They wanted to make sure it was okay to make a big deal of Peggy's success and to savor every moment of her pleasure. I reassured them that when it comes to homework, parents can't be too enthusiastic, and that in addition to giving Peggy a reward, they should continue letting Peggy know how pleased they were.

- **Is your child feeling better about herself?** A lot of things that happen when your child plays the Behavior Game should help her feel good about herself. Most important, by praising your child for her good behavior, she should begin to feel better about herself. Children who hear about the good things they do instead of the bad, learn to believe in themselves. They gradually recognize that they can do worthwhile things; that they're not always messing up. As they get used to hearing their parents say good things to them, they start saying good things to themselves. You can hope, and expect, that this change will be happening to your child.

Let's look at the development of Adam, the son of my clients Trudie and Jeff Eastman.

The first time eight-year-old Adam Eastman and I talked, he made it clear that he felt as if the whole world was against him and that he couldn't do anything right. What made him feel worse, he told me, was that his younger sister Terry was "perfect." No one ever yelled at her or criticized her. But the moment he did even the littlest thing wrong, boom, his parents were all over him.

Before the Game, Adam saw himself in negative terms and felt pretty bad about himself. But once I helped his parents, Trudie and Jeff, get the

Game started, their praise and encouragement made Adam feel better about himself. The positive feedback he was getting from his parents helped Adam acknowledge the good things he did, such as taking care of his cat, coming home on time, and helping out when asked. After several weeks of playing the Game, Adam confided in me that maybe he wasn't so bad after all and that his parents had become a lot nicer to be around.

•   **Is your child better able to manage his anger?**   Over time, playing the Behavior Game should help your child stay in control of himself when he gets upset. Teaching your child different ways to "cool off" when he's angry will help him calm down and avoid overreacting to situations. In addition, discipline techniques such as time-out and the quiet chair should encourage your child to think before acting impulsively.

Let's see how time-out helped my clients Jerry and Clara Hildebrand's children to cut down on their fighting.

After playing the Game for six weeks, Charlie, age ten, shared with me how he "really" felt about time-out: "Doctor, I hate that time-out. Sitting in my room is so boring." He went on to tell me that every time he got in a fight with his little sister Gwen, his mom sent him to his room. And what made him feel worse was that his mom didn't seem to care whose fault the fight was, he still had to go to his room. We talked about what Charlie could do to avoid time-out in the future. After thinking for a moment, Charlie reluctantly came up with the answer—he had to get along better with Gwen. We agreed that this was a tall order, because Gwen was always teasing him, but that maybe by putting our heads together we could come up with a plan for Charlie. Next time Gwen started bothering him, he'd try to keep his mouth shut, remember how much he didn't like time-out, let Gwen know that he wouldn't play with her until she quit teasing him, and leave the situation.

The next week when I saw the whole family together, everyone was abuzz with what a great week it had been because Charlie and Gwen had hardly fought at all. When I asked them why they thought this happened, Charlie told me that our plan had worked—instead of fighting, he'd told Gwen to cool it with the teasing or he wouldn't play with her anymore. Clara confirmed this and added that whenever a fight was about to begin, Charlie left the room. At this point Charlie nodded. "I told you I could do it, Doctor. I told you I could do whatever it took to keep from getting a time-out." I congratulated Charlie on his victory and let him know how proud I was of his determination.

In time your child should discover how to avoid having a time-out just like Charlie did. When this happens don't be surprised if you catch your child giving herself her own warnings to stop doing whatever usually sends her for time-out, whether it's fighting with a brother, flying into a rage, or having to start her homework.

To get an idea about how well your child's doing controlling his behavior, review how often you're disciplining your child now compared with one or two months ago. If your child isn't going for time-out as often, isn't getting privileges taken away as much, and/or isn't being put on restriction as frequently, then he's improving and learning to control his behavior.

• **Does your child seem happier and more content?** When a child experiences her parents as encouraging, supportive helpers, she's calmer and happier. When she doesn't worry as much about making mistakes and getting criticized for trying things, she feels less anxious.

When a child feels as if his home is a place where promises are kept, he feels secure. By now, your child knows that when you say something, you're likely to mean it and follow through, whether it's with a reward for good behavior or a discipline technique for problem behavior. Over time, this kind of follow-through helps to build trust and respect between you and your child.

Making good on your word creates an atmosphere of predictability and stability where words and actions are related. In a world where there's so much unpredictability, if your child can experience some certainty at home and be surrounded by parents whom she can count on to do what they say, and who will try to be fair and understanding, she'll develop confidence in herself, which is nice. Playing the Behavior Game can go a long way in helping create and maintain this kind of atmosphere.

Of course, playing the Behavior Game won't remove all the stress from your child's life. That would be impossible and undesirable—it's not realistic for your child to go through life wearing rose-tinted glasses. Still, it's nice if she can enjoy herself at least some of the time as she grows up.

DECIDING WHETHER YOUR CHILD NEEDS MORE HELP

Although my clients and their children benefit significantly from playing the Game, sometimes we need to do more. So keep in mind that no matter how good a job you're doing and how hard you're trying, your child may have problems that the Behavior Game alone won't solve.

Suppose after playing the Game for six to eight weeks, you've taken stock and decided that your child isn't making the progress you had hoped for, particularly with certain troublesome kinds of behavior. At this point, you might want to think about getting some extra help. Don't feel bad if your child needs extra guidance; most children need special assistance from time to time. Some problems can't be solved without special help.

In my clinical experience, since each child and each situation is unique, there are no hard-and-fast rules about when you should or shouldn't pursue outside help. To help you make your decision, I've included some examples of what happened as my clients and I pondered getting extra help for their children. As you'll see sometimes we simply gave the problem more time to go away, other times we fine-tuned the Game a bit, and still other times we reached out to other professionals in the community. I hope that the following scenarios will provide you with guidance as you consider whether or not to get extra help for your child.

• **Your child continues to have significant difficulties with schoolwork.** Perhaps your child can't concentrate long enough to finish his assignments, or even though he tries he still can't learn the material. Certain subjects such as reading or math may be especially difficult for him. If you suspect that your child may have a learning problem, share your concerns with his teacher and school counselor and ask for their help. They may recommend testing to determine what is interfering with your child's ability to learn or individual tutoring that focuses on the problems your child is having.

Let's see how my client Janet used these ideas to get some additional help for her son Seth.

Although Janet had been playing the Game for a few weeks, using short study periods didn't seem to be helping her seven-year-old son Seth to sit down and read for more than a few minutes. She was getting more and more frustrated, especially because this approach was working well with her older daughter, Patty, age ten. She asked me if something was the matter with Seth and why wasn't the Game working for him? To clarify what was happening, Janet and I met with Seth's teacher and school counselor. Together we decided that it would be a good idea if the school psychologist gave Seth a few tests to double-check his reading level and to determine whether he had any perceptual problems with seeing the letters or sounding them out. The tests revealed that although Seth had no learning disabilities, his reading level was below grade level. The school psychologist recommended individual tutoring twice a week for at least the next several months. After several weeks of tutoring in reading, Seth began to show improvement. Janet shared her relief with me about having taken a first step to help Seth with his reading and that it was working.

• **Your child is overly obstinate, stubborn, and oppositional.**   Although most children go through periods of being self-centered and impossible to get along with, if your child always refuses to talk to and/or get along with you and the rest of the family, she may benefit from getting some outside help. If in spite of your attempts to play the Game with your child, she seems incapable of making any compromises and insists on getting her own way no matter what, consider getting some professional advice from your pediatrician or a mental health counselor on how to help her.

Let's see what my clients the Dunns did in this situation.

Judy Dunn, age twelve, and her parents Stephanie and Derrick were constantly fighting over something. It seemed as if Judy always wanted her own way and was never willing to compromise. Before the Game Stephanie and Derrick usually gave in to their daughter in order to avoid a blowup. Now, with the Game, they were standing their ground, rewarding compliance, and setting limits. Although these techniques had helped considerably, they still didn't feel as though they could really communicate with Judy. As patient as they tried to be, Judy would set them off, and their attempts to talk and listen would go up in smoke. Together we decided that the whole family should meet with me to work specifically on communication. In addition, I would meet individually with Judy to give her a chance to tell me her side of the story and to help her learn how to compromise and be more flexible. The first few weeks were rocky, but gradually by working together, everyone was able to get along better.

• **Your child is unhappy, moody, and sad most of the time.** Most children are happy at least some of the time and able to enjoy themselves. However, some children become very depressed and need immediate medical and/or psychological help. If your child acts as if he hates himself, repeatedly says horrible things about himself, and cries all the time, don't wait to get help. See your child's doctor as soon as possible.

Let's see what my clients Linda and Doug O'Neill did when they realized their daughter's mood had suddenly and dramatically changed.

Although initially Samantha, age ten, had responded positively to the Game, her mother Linda confided in me that in the last several weeks something had changed. Since Samantha seemed down-in-the-dumps, Linda and Doug had done everything they could think of to cheer her up. Linda took her shopping and bought her a new outfit and her current favorite compact disk. Doug spent extra time with her. But nothing helped. She didn't even seem happy when her friends came over to play. Linda and I agreed that something must be wrong with Sam. When Sam came to talk to me, she told me she didn't know why but she was tired and sad all the time. Sam's mood worried me. As a first step I recommended Sam visit her pediatrician for a checkup to determine whether there were any physical problems that might be contributing to Sam's mood. A physical exam and lab test revealed that Sam had a hormonal imbalance. By prescribing medication and following her progress closely, Sam's pediatrician was able to help Sam regain her enthusiasm and cheerful spirit.

As a final note on this subject, if your child seems depressed, take her seriously. Children do not want to be depressed. Although you should expect your child to be down-in-the-dumps occasionally, if your child is sad most of the time, especially when good things are happening, don't hesitate; get some help. I recommend that you start by contacting your child's pediatrician. Share your concerns with the doctor and ask for advice on what to do.

- **Your child is anxious, shy, and/or fearful much of the time in a variety of situations.**   It can be very hard for a parent to deal with a child who is afraid to try anything new and often seems almost paralyzed by fear. If your child clings to you and seems scared of everything, talk to your child's doctor or counselor about how he can be helped. Keep in mind that frequently this kind of problem will improve if you are patient and introduce your child to change very gradually.

Let's see how my client Vicky Wentworth went the extra mile to help her son Vince.

Vicky told me that she had not expected her son Vince to be so timid and emotional. His older sister Veronica was very independent. Even on her first day of kindergarten, Veronica had been raring to go. She couldn't wait to meet her teacher and classmates. But Vince had been quite different. He had cried and cried when Vicki left him in class on his first day. Although Vicki recognized that Vince would probably never be as outgoing as his sister, she wanted to help him feel more comfortable at school. So in addition to rewarding good behavior at home, Vicky and I expanded the Game to include a reward for going to school without crying, for saying good-bye to his mother, and for walking into the classroom. This addition to the Game made it much easier for Vince to go to school. However, once at school, he continued to be timid and shy. As a precaution, I suggested that Vicky and I meet with Vince's kindergarten teacher to explore ways to help make Vince's adjustment easier. His teacher told us that she had several other students who were having a tough time and encouraged Vicky to give Vince another month to settle in. This extra time seemed to be just right for Vince. Gradually he made some friends and even told his mom that sometimes school was fun, especially when he got to paint and color.

- **Your child has no friends and most other children dislike her.**   In spite of your efforts if your child just can't make friends and is miserable because no one likes her, it's a good idea to get input from other adults who spend time around her to find out what she's doing that is turning the other children off and what can be done to help her.

Let's see what happened when my client Juanita Hernandez used these suggestions.

Juanita beamed with pride as she told me about her six-year-old daughter Sally. Sally was very responsible, a natural leader who loved being in charge. Sally was very motivated by the Behavior Game and had shown considerable improvement at home. But at school, especially at recess, she was still having problems getting along with the other children. Juanita was concerned that the other children were avoiding her daughter because she was too bossy. Juanita and I decided she should meet with Sally's teacher, Mr. Gelb, and share her concerns. Mr. Gelb was very understanding and helpful. He offered to talk with Sally and suggested that he and Sally come up with a secret signal to use when she was getting too bossy. When he saw Sally being too bossy, he'd let her know by scratching his head. Since Sally wanted her classmates to like her, this signal worked out well. In no time, Mr. Gelb was hardly scratching his head at all and Sally was enjoying playing with her classmates.

• **Your child has a lot of out-of-control and/or violent temper tantrums.** Although all children lose their tempers from time to time, if your child loses control frequently over even the smallest things, ask his pediatrician or a mental health professional about getting guidance in how to help him with his impulsiveness and lack of control.

Let's see what advice I gave my client Sarah Parker on how to deal with her son's temper tantrums.

"Why does Kevin get so upset over everything and start screaming and crying? His older brother and sister weren't like this. What's the matter with Kevin? How can I help him?" Sarah asked me in desperation. From her description of her four-year-old son, Kevin seemed to be one of those children who was prewired to fly off the handle easily. I recommended that as a first step, Sarah give the Behavior Game a try. In particular I suggested that Kevin would benefit if he could earn rewards for staying in control when things weren't going his way. In addition, Sarah should give him a warning and then send him for a time-out when a tantrum was beginning. And even though he was only four, Sarah should try to use the discussion times to talk to Kevin briefly about things that were upsetting him. Eventually, this would help Kevin learn to use words instead of always screaming and crying to express his frustrations. If these ideas hadn't helped after several weeks, Sarah and I would put our heads together and consider other options such as a consultation with his pediatrician about any possible physical problems that might be contributing to Kevin's outbursts.

• **Your child frequently tells big lies, steals, cheats, or gets in dangerous fights.**   Every child makes up stories from time to time and has fights with other children; however, if your child is lying to you, taking things that don't belong to him, or threatening and intimidating other children, I recommend that you seek advice from your pediatrician or a mental health professional about how to deal with this behavior before it gets out of control.

Let's see what my clients the Keefers did to help their son stop bullying and fighting.

Whitney Keefer was big and strong for his age. Although only five he had already learned how powerful he was, especially on the playground. One mean look could make the other children run away. Concerned that Whitney would become a bully, his mom Cheryl sought my help. As a first step I recommended that Cheryl put the Behavior Game into action at home. By getting rewards for behavior that was the opposite of fighting, such as playing nicely with his sisters and friends and by being sent for time-out when he started to fight, Whitney improved considerably at home. To help Whitney at school, I recommended we meet with his preschool teacher for her ideas about how to bring his playground behavior under control. His teacher and aide liked the idea of a playground Game that rewarded Whitney for playing nicely and provided a warning and then an immediate time-out for any kind of bullying. Although he didn't like being benched, Whitney responded very well to these strict and immediate limits. His fighting decreased and he learned that there were other ways to act around his classmates.

As a final caution, remember that there are no universal rules on when to ask for help. Some parents rarely seek assistance; others get help frequently. In general, when you're worried about your child, don't keep it to yourself. Share your concerns with a friend who can offer you kindness and understanding. And as a rule, it's always a good idea to consult with your child's pediatrician first when you have a concern about your child. He or she is aware of your child's developmental history and can help you evaluate current problems and find any necessary help.

No matter where you go for help, keep in mind that pediatricians, teachers, school counselors, psychologists, social workers, and other professionals are there to provide services for you and your child. Don't feel uncomfortable or think that you're inappropriately taking up someone's time. When you have a question, let them do their jobs by giving you an answer.

If you decide to get extra help be selective in who you choose to help you. It's important that you work with people with whom you feel comfortable and can trust to do the right thing. Always let the person you're working with know that you've been playing the Behavior Game and make sure they understand how it works. And don't stop the Behavior Game unless the professional who is helping you advises it. Usually continuing to play the Behavior Game makes other types of help even more successful, whether it's medication, counseling, therapy, testing, or tutoring.

If you feel your child needs professional help, please refer to Appendix C, which lists general guidelines and agencies you can contact in your search for guidance and assistance.

LOOKING AHEAD TO THE FUTURE

I consider the Behavior Game to work best for children from ages two to twelve; teenagers are another matter altogether. As your children get older, here are some tips for making sure the good you've accomplished together remains intact, whether or not you continue to play the Game "officially."

• **Keep using encouragement, praise, and rewards.** Although someday you may stop using a chart and putting up stars or check marks, you should never quit using the basics of the Game.

Make rewarding good behavior a habit you carry with you forever. Don't fall into the trap of taking good behavior for granted. If you stop letting your child know what a good job she's doing, she may stop doing such a good job.

You may always need to give some kind of earned reward for certain kinds of good behavior. Many parents find that no matter how old their child is, they still need to reward doing chores and schoolwork to make sure this good behavior continues.

Make sure everyone, including you, has something good—a treat or a goal—to anticipate. Whether or not you're still using a formal Game, your family still needs to have things to look forward to. Plan pleasant and fun things for the family to do together.

• **Don't lose touch with your child.**   Continue your times for discussing their daily experiences, and stay in contact with your child. No matter how busy you are, spend some time each day talking with your child. If no one feels like talking, do something everyone enjoys. Most children like these discussions as long as they are relaxed and no demands are made.

Let's see how my client Rosalinda Saldana fit time for sharing the day's happenings with her daughter Delia into her busy schedule.

Even though her family seemed to be on the go from morning to night, Rosalinda was determined to spend some time every day talking with and listening to her six-year-old daughter Delia. Some days the only time they had was in the car driving to and from school. Other days, Rosalinda invited Delia to run errands with her. As they were shopping for food or picking up the dry cleaning, Rosalinda asked Delia about her day and offered her support. And, to sweeten the pot, she usually let Delia pick out a treat for being so helpful while they were doing errands. Rosalinda's efforts paid off. Delia felt comfortable talking to her mom, especially when things were bothering her, because she could count on Rosalinda's support and help.

• **Treat your child as the unique and special person she is.**   Don't lose sight of your child's own particular mix of things she does well and things she doesn't. Don't fall into the trap of comparing your child to other children.

Each child has his own developmental timetable. Your child may develop quickly in one area but not in another. Or, he may develop slowly in almost all areas. Each child is different. Don't push or expect too much, too soon. Give your child the time, patience, and encouragement he needs to develop at his own speed. Growing up requires gradually mastering a series of skills. Make sure you're going slow and showing your child how to do the new things he needs to do.

Let's see how my client Olivia Masters coped with her two very different children, Jamal and Kesha.

Talk about two ends of the continuum—Jamal did everything developmentally ahead of schedule. He was walking before one year and never stopped babbling from the moment he was born. His sister Kesha was just the opposite. She seemed to take her sweet time doing everything. When would Kesha talk, Olivia wondered. I encouraged Olivia to be patient and reassured her that there was probably nothing wrong with Kesha that a little time wouldn't fix. I also suggested she get a second opinion by talking with her daughter's pediatrician. Getting his perspective eased Olivia's mind. The doctor agreed with me that at this point there was no cause for alarm and that what Kesha needed most was her mother's continued patience and support. It took a while, but finally Kesha started talking, so much in fact, that Olivia joked about the good old days when the house was relatively quiet and her children didn't argue all the time.

• **Give stubborn problems extra time to go away.**   With long-standing bad habits, don't resort to physical punishment; instead try giving longer time-outs, or taking away special privileges or setting up short restrictions. In addition, you can reward improvement of these chronic problems with something special. For example, if your child has a long history of homework problems, you may need to offer the reward of staying up later only if she completes her schoolwork. Once it sinks in that the only way to stay up later is by doing her schoolwork, your child is likely to get to work.

• **Don't throw in the towel.**   If you have an awful day or a horrible week, don't give up. Remember that every family has a truly terrible day from time to time. When it happens in your family, be as calm as you can and don't overreact. Sometimes you won't be able to help yourself, and before you know it you'll be screaming, yelling, pouting, withdrawing, or stomping around. When this happens, be sure to apologize to your family, explain why you blew up, wipe the slate clean, and keep the Game going. Don't dwell on awful days. Acknowledge them, try to learn from them, and then leave them in the past where they belong.

Let's see how my client Roberto coped with an all-too-typical bad day.

What a day it had been for Roberto, Juan and Anita's father. Nothing had gone right at his job and someone almost crashed into him on the drive home. So when he saw his children's bikes in the driveway again, he lost it. As they heard their dad screaming from the car, Juan and Anita knew they were in trouble. Running outside, they got their bikes out of the way in record speed. But that didn't seem to calm their dad down. He was still furious as he stormed into the house and barked, "How can you two be so irresponsible and thoughtless? Can't you even remember to put your bikes away? Isn't that simple enough? You're grounded. No television or friends for a month." At this point Juan and Anita retreated to their rooms. Their dad needed a chance to calm down. At dinner, Roberto explained to them that he'd had a bad day and that their bikes were the final straw. But now that he'd had time to think about it, he realized that he'd over-reacted and that restriction didn't seem like the right thing to do. Together they agreed that if they left their bikes in the driveway again they'd lose the chance to use them for the next day. Having patched things up, Roberto regrouped, and much to his surprise had a pleasant evening with his children. After Roberto shared this story with me, I congratulated him on being able to apologize to his children and make amends for "losing it." I let him know that every parent overreacts from time to time and that the most important thing is to acknowledge this and set the record straight.

• **No matter how well the Game goes, don't expect everyone to love it.** There always seems to be at least one relative or friend who just can't accept the Game. Your child's grandmother may insist that Game is wrong because you're bribing your child to do things he should want to do on his own. Your child's uncle may insist that you're spoiling your child with rewards and not being strict enough. Your neighbor may insist that children shouldn't get encouragement or support as that weakens them. Whatever the naysayers claim, stick to your guns. Ignore them or change the subject. Remember, you know what is best for your child and you're doing it. That's what counts.

• **Keep your sense of humor.**   Although parenting without the Behavior Game is difficult, I find that parenting without a sense of humor is impossible. Finding something funny is a great way to keep things in perspective. So try to lighten up and encourage your family to laugh a little.

• **And finally, never forget that the Behavior Game can be a close friend of the family, always there ready to help out when needed.**   Even if you quit using the Game for a while, you can always start it up again, and it will work. So as time goes by don't forget about it. Keep it in the back of your mind, and if and when you need it again, get it started and watch it help.

CELEBRATING YOUR VICTORIES

This section is included to alert you to the importance of formally acknowledging your family's accomplishments. I've worked with far too many families who didn't think they really deserved to celebrate because things could still be better. Even though you may have many more goals you're striving toward, you and your family deserve a pat on the back for your efforts. If nothing else, your time, effort, and patience deserve some official recognition. And what about your children? They've hung in there and made a go of it. They should be in line for some congratulations as well. So it's highly recommended that sometime after your "taking stock" review, you celebrate your success with the Game.

Make your celebration as simple or complicated as you want, but be sure to plan something that everyone will enjoy. Many families I've worked with have staged a special family party. Sometimes only the immediate family was invited; other times relatives and even friends participated. Whatever kind of party you plan, try to get the whole family involved from the beginning. Make it a real family affair. In case any inspiration is needed, let's look in on the Bradleys as they plan their party.

As soon as Cindy and Bobby heard about the party that was planned, they could think of little else. Cindy declared herself decoration and entertainment chairman and suggested her mom Joan be in charge of the food. After discussing almost every kind of food there was, the following menu was agreed upon: Bobby chose pizza and ice cream; Cindy wanted lemonade and cookies as well. Joan included a salad and some fruit. Gary voted for chips and salsa.

Cindy and Bobby went to the store with Joan and picked out paper plates and napkins with stars, moons, and suns on them. Using markers and stickers, they made a poster that congratulated the whole family on their accomplishments. They spent several days creating entertainment for the party. Cindy decided to do a kind of before-and-after skit about the Behavior Game. Although she had warned her parents that this was coming, they were hardly prepared for the production that Cindy and Bobby staged.

The party began with snacks and the entertainment. Bobby, acting as usher, sat Joan and Gary down and told them to close their eyes and not open them until Cindy said so. This accomplished, Cindy and Bobby got into their costumes. Cindy dressed as Joan and Bobby as Gary began their reenactment.

Cindy, playing the part of Joan, did a send-up of her mother, first showing Joan doing everything wrong, yelling at her children and threatening them with no more television. Bobby intervened and in his sternest Gary voice warned the children that if they didn't shape up they'd have to stay in their rooms forever. Everyone was laughing as Gary asked, "Are we still like that?" Cindy and Bobby responded with a resounding, "No way!" and proceeded to role-play the new, improved Joan and Gary, complete with rewarding comments, encouragement, and praise.

After repeated curtain calls and several standing ovations, Gary brought out a surprise for his family. He'd had special T-shirts made to honor each family member. Each shirt had a name, *Cindy*, *Bobby*, *Mom*, or *Dad* and then said, "is an official winner of the Behavior Game."

They all loved their "winner" T-shirts, and put them on. After that, hugs, kisses, and thank-yous were shared by everyone. It was a perfect time for a family portrait.

As the party was breaking up, Cindy and Bobby began to worry. Since they had their winner T-shirts, did that mean the Game was over and that they wouldn't get to play it anymore? In a panic they asked their parents if the Game was over. Joan quickly reassured them that the Game would go on. Breathing a sigh of relief, Bobby and Cindy began thinking of all the rewards they'd be earning in the future.

Just as the Bradleys did, you'll probably find you want to keep playing the Game with your child. And to make sure your Game stays current and meets your family's ever-changing needs, the last chapter provides you with guidelines for revising the Game throughout the year.

9

KEEPING THE GAME UP-TO-DATE THROUGHOUT THE YEAR

In addition to renewing the Game from week to week, it's a good idea to pause periodically and do a big-picture checkup to make sure that the Game is continuing to meet your family's ever-changing needs.

Most of the families I work with benefit from doing this kind of checkup three times a year. Doing a thorough overview in the fall as school is starting, in the winter when the new year begins, and at the beginning of summer when school is over can help you make sure your Game stays current. As you begin your checkup, review your child's Game and be sure to get his ideas about changes that should be made. Each big-picture checkup can have its own special focus. In the fall you can concentrate on school and extracurricular activities. You can use your winter review to spend extra time double-checking on how the various aspects of your Behavior Game are working. And when school is ending, you can develop a Game that's more relaxed and just right for summer vacation.

Once you've decided on any needed changes, use your regularly scheduled weekly meeting to talk with your child about her new Game and get it started. And then for the next several weeks, carefully monitor your child's Game to make sure it's functioning as it should.

You may want to skim over this chapter quickly and later when the time is right, you can go over the appropriate sections in detail. The following three sections contain suggestions to help you do your fall, winter, and summer checkups.

169

YOUR FALL CHECKUP

My clients find that school opening is a good time for a checkup. During this review you and your child will be putting together his back-to-school Behavior Game, deciding what extracurricular activities he'll be participating in, and talking about all the changes that will be happening when school starts.

Preparing Your Fall Game

Here are some tips to follow as you plan your child's back-to-school Game:

• **Begin your checkup one or two weeks before school starts.**   Don't wait until the last minute to begin your fall checkup. Give yourself plenty of time. Of the three big-picture checkups you do, this is likely to be the most difficult and time consuming because of all the changes that going back to school requires.

• **Together with your child go over his Good Behavior Chart and decide on what changes are necessary.**   During the summer, if you relaxed your standards for good behavior, you'll probably need to change them back to the way they were during the previous school year. As you're looking over the kinds of behavior on her chart, keep a special eye out for any behavior that was a problem during the summer, and make sure you keep working on it.

• **Set wake-up time and bedtime.**   Often, families get up later and go to bed later in the summer. If your family did this, it's time to set both an earlier get-up time and an earlier bedtime.

• **Allow adequate time for studying and homework.**   As you have before, you'll be using the game to encourage your child to do his schoolwork. During the summer he may have gotten out of the habit of sitting down and paying attention. During the first few weeks of school, plan to help him get used to studying and doing his schoolwork again.

Keep in mind that until school actually starts, you won't know how much schoolwork your child will be doing, so you may need to wait until you know more before setting up the specifics of "doing homework."

• **Choose extracurricular activities.**   It's important to spend time talking with your child about the activities she wants to do and then deciding on the ones she'll be involved in during the coming months. It can be easy for a child to take on too many activities. When you're picking out the things she's going to do, try to be sensitive to how much your child can handle and make sure she's not overloaded. Children with too many activities often get stressed out, their schoolwork suffers, and they're tired and unhappy.

Choose one or two activities you want him to participate in, and one or two activities he finds interesting. Make sure your child understands why you think the activities you're asking him to do are important. To encourage him to do these activities you may want to include them on his chart and offer check marks or stars for doing them.

When you and your child are choosing activities, you may find that you disagree. You may want her to do something that she doesn't want to do, such as taking music lessons, going to religion class, or being tutored. And she may want to do things you don't feel are as important. If this happens, you need to compromise.

Throughout the coming months carefully monitor your child's extracurricular activities. From time to time, check with your child to find out how his activities are going. If he seems too busy and unable to get his schoolwork done, he's probably trying to do too much and needs to cut back. On the other hand, if you feel that your child can handle what he's doing, encourage him to stick with the activity until he's had time to see how he likes it. Making your child stay involved in an activity for the season or the year can help teach him about commitment and following through.

• **Double-check your child's Reward Chart.**   Talk with your child and find out if she still likes her rewards. As your child gets older she may want the chance to earn more money or more free time. She may want to save up for something special.

• **Make up your child's fall Game.**   Once you and your child have agreed on his good behavior and rewards, fill out a revised Good Behavior Chart and Reward Chart. Have these charts ready for your fall checkup meeting.

• **Preview the new school year.**   Throughout your preparation, try to spend some time talking about what will be happening during the next few months. The start of school means a new teacher, some different classmates, perhaps some new activities, and uncertainty about what's going to happen.

Some children have more problems adjusting to these changes than others. If your child tends to be hesitant about doing new things, make sure to spend extra time going over what will be happening once school starts. It's often a good idea to do this a little bit at a time. Maybe talk about it for five to ten minutes each day when your child is willing to listen. Talking about it any longer than that can make your child feel overwhelmed and scared.

You may want to share with your child the worries you had as a child about new things, such as school starting and not knowing what was going to happen. Knowing you had worries, too, when you were his age will usually make your child feel better. Also, your child will be able to handle the uncertainty more easily if you remind him that you'll be there standing behind him and helping him get adjusted.

If your child is starting school for the first time or going to a new school, spend extra time talking about how this might feel. If you haven't already done so, visit the school, meet the teachers, go into a classroom, and walk around the campus. Try to meet some other children who are going to the school. Help your child get as familiar as she can with this new situation.

Getting Started

To make sure you get off on the right foot, here are some guidelines to follow as you begin your fall Game:

• **Have an official back-to-school checkup meeting.** After you've finished planning for the fall, it's a good idea to use your regular Sunday family meeting to talk about your child's new back-to-school Game and how it will work. In a way, this meeting officially marks the end of vacation and the beginning of school. The Sunday before school starts is often the best time for this meeting. If this time seems too close to the start of school, have the meeting a week before.

• **Talk about what happened during the summer.** Encourage all family members to talk about what they did and what they enjoyed during their vacation. Make sure all of your children get recognition for the good things they did or the progress they made during the summer, whether it was playing sports, doing a job, helping out at home, working on a skill like math or reading, or participating in any other activity. Some of my clients, especially those with older children, also use this part of the meeting to talk about problems that occurred over the last several months and how they plan to address them in the near future. If you feel this kind of discussion would be helpful to your family, you can include it here as well.

• **Go over the revised Game and how it will work.** As you review your child's good behavior and rewards, pay special attention to any changes that have been made. Be sure to go over the activities your child is going to be involved in.

- **Encourage your family to work together.** It's a good idea to remind everyone that schedules will get more hectic as school begins. The entire family will benefit if everyone pulls together and helps one another. That way all of them can be ready on time, get where they have to go, and have time to do the things that need to get done.

Keep in mind that the schedule you make is meant to help you and your family, so be flexible and don't become a prisoner of your schedule. Be prepared to change it as often as necessary.

- **Put your child's chart up and start playing.** Just as you have every other week, put your child's Good Behavior Chart and his Reward Chart up on the refrigerator and give him a chance to begin earning stars or check marks.

- **End the meeting on a positive note.** Let your child know how much you're looking forward to the next several months. Have your child tell you about something she's looking forward to. Finish the meeting with a special treat, or later in the day have a special dinner or perhaps even go out for dinner.

- **Give your child time to adjust to his new Game.** To help your child become familiar with the changes you made, give him reminders and advance notices. Once he's used to his new chart, you can decrease these reminders. Keep talking with and listening to your child about all the new things that are going on. Watch carefully and make sure your child's Game is working.

- **Be flexible.** No matter how thoroughly you prepare, it's impossible to predict everything that will happen. Don't be surprised if you need to make changes in your child's Game. As you find out more about the demands of her school and activities schedule, you can change the Game and your family's routine to accommodate these requirements.

Let's see what happened when my clients Simone and Denzel Andrews did their fall checkup for their sixth-grade son Noah and their third-grade daughter Taylor.

Since Noah always put a lot of pressure on himself and tended to over-commit, Simone and Denzel were determined to help him develop a back-to-school Game that wouldn't be overwhelming. Noah would have to choose only one sport at a time and only one after-school activity. Noah decided on soccer and booster club. That left time for doing schoolwork, chores, and having friends over. His younger sister was different from Noah. If given free rein, Taylor would spend hours by herself in her room, reading or creating something. When planning her fall Game, Simone and Denzel encouraged her to get involved in an activity that included other children. After much discussion, Taylor choose an art class that met two afternoons a week. Since Taylor had shown little interest in math, her parents also planned to watch her school progress carefully and if necessary get her some tutoring in math.

YOUR WINTER CHECKUP

Your next big-picture checkup is scheduled for winter as the new year is beginning, so when the winter holidays are approaching, you can begin to plan. During this checkup you can take extra time to review how the Game has gone since school began and take a close look at what's working and what isn't. This review will help you decide what you want to keep and what you want to change for the upcoming winter and spring months.

Preparing for Your Winter Game

Here are some tips to follow as you prepare your child's winter Game:

- **Begin your checkup when the winter holidays are ending.** Remember that this checkup isn't likely to be as thorough or as time consuming as your fall checkup. A quick review of your child's progress during the fall and perhaps making a few minor changes may be all you want to do.
- **Together with your child, go over his Good Behavior Chart and decide on needed changes.** You may decide to keep everything the same. If you feel that the Game is working well and that your child is making progress, you may decide that there's no reason to make a change.

On the other hand, you may decide to make some changes. As they double-check their child's chart, some of the families I work with find that during the fall they gradually let up on playing the Game and become too relaxed. If this has happened to you, the winter checkup offers you the perfect time to re-group, tighten things up, and restart the Game.

• **Find ways to tighten up your Game.**   This involves going back to the basics. It means following through with each part of your child's Behavior Game. It means using reminders more often, rewarding behavior more promptly and consistently, making sure cash-in times occur, and being certain your discipline plan is carried out.

• **Focus on a continuing problem.**   Some families also use this checkup as a time to redouble their efforts to help their child with a chronic problem, such as not getting along with others, not doing what is asked, or not completing his homework. Consider creating a special reward to help your child overcome his chronic problem. If he can't remember to bring his schoolwork home, offer him a special reward when he does. If he can't seem to get along with his brother, offer him extra free time if he shows improvement. Whatever his long-standing difficulty, try to find a special reward that motivates him to change.

• **Eliminate or add activities.**   Now is a good time to take a hard look at your child's activities and together decide if any of them need to be dropped or new ones added. Talk with your child about her activities and find out how she feels about them. If they seem to be overwhelming her or interfering with other things she has to do, you may need to discontinue some of them. If there's something you want her to try, discuss this as well.

• **Revise your daily schedule.**   If your family doesn't have enough time in the morning to get ready, set an earlier wake-up time. If there's not enough time to do homework, rearrange things. If your child can't get ready for bed on time, have him start earlier. As a rule allow your child too much rather than too little time to get things done.

• **Review your child's Reward Chart.**   Talk with your child about her rewards. Find out how she feels about them and if she wants to add any or change any.

• **Make up your child's winter Game.**   Once you've gathered all this information about behavior and rewards, fill out a revised Good Behavior Chart and Reward Chart that includes the changes you made. Have it ready for your winter checkup meeting.

Getting Started

To help you get going again, here are some tips to follow as you put your new Game into action:

- **Have an official winter checkup meeting.**   After you've done your review, use your regular Sunday meeting to talk about how the Game will work for the next several months. Since this meeting signals that it's time to go back to school, try to have the meeting the Sunday before school begins again.
- **Talk about what happened during the fall.**   Encourage the whole family to spend some time going over what they did during the last several months, especially the positive things they were involved in. Ask your child to share some of his favorite stories. Give your child recognition for any progress he made during the fall.
- **Go over the revised Game and how it will work.**   As you're going over the Game, spend extra time on the behavior and rewards that have been changed. If you tightened up on some kind of behavior, review with your child why and how you did this. If you're planning to pay extra attention to a certain kind of behavior, discuss this with your child as well. Go over the activities your child is involved in. Run through your schedule for the coming months.
- **Put up your child's chart and start playing.**   Just as you have every other week, put your child's chart up on the refrigerator and have her get started.
- **Do something fun at the end of the meeting.**   Remember how you ended your fall meeting on a positive note? Do the same thing after this meeting. Have a favorite snack or a favorite dinner, or go out to dinner.
- **Watch carefully and make sure your revised Game is working**.   Just as you did in the fall, during the first few weeks keep an eye on the behavior you tightened up on. If you are focusing on a certain kind of behavior, such as getting along or doing schoolwork, pay extra attention to it as well. And as you have before, give your child time to adjust to any changes in the Game.

Let's see how my clients Sue and Lee Tashiro fared during their winter checkup:

Although pleased with eight-year-old Alec's fall Game, Sue and Lee wanted to make a few changes. Alec did not like wearing his new reading glasses because the other children teased him. To encourage him to use his glasses, Sue and Lee decided on using a special daily reward. For each day he wore his glasses, Alec would earn video game points. In two or three weeks he'd have enough points to buy himself a game. Sue and Lee also made sure to listen and offer support when Alec told them how the other children hurt his feelings when they teased him about his glasses. After a while, as Alec was able to tune them out and ignore them, he discovered that his class-mates almost never called him "four eyes" anymore.

YOUR SUMMER CHECKUP

When summer vacation is a few weeks away, begin to plan your summer checkup. During the summer, even though your child is on vacation and has fewer responsibilities, it's still a good idea to continue playing the Game and following some kind of routine. Many parents make up a relaxed Game to use during the summer. If your child will be in day care or day camp during the summer, try to find a program that's fun and relaxing but provides some opportunity for learning as well.

Preparing Your Summer Game

Let's take a look at some guidelines you can follow when you're planning your child's summer Game.

• **Begin your summer checkup a week or two before school ends.**   As school is coming to a close and everyone is gearing up for vacation, you can begin planning your vacation Game.

• **Together with your child, go over his Good Behavior Chart and decide any necessary changes.**   In general you may want to relax some of the re-quirements for good behavior, while leaving the other requirements the same. You may also want to add special summer behavior involving chores, educa-tional activities, or something your child needs to work on.

• **Relax your daily schedule.**   You may want to make wake-up time a little later and give your child more time to get ready in the morning. In the evening, you may want to set a later bedtime and give everyone more time to get ready for bed and to talk, play games, or watch television before bed.

Even though it's summertime, not lowering your standards for getting along with one another and doing what is asked is important. Don't let the vacation become a time when your children fight with one another even more or get into the bad habit of talking back to you.

• **Add chores or create a "summer job."**   Some parents want their children to help them out more in the summer and therefore increase the number of chores their children can do to earn stars or check marks. You may want to consider this idea if you feel your child is ready to help you out more around the house. If your child is old enough, you may want to offer him the chance to perform a "job" during the summer, such as helping you take care of a younger brother or sister, being in charge of a pet, or taking some other kind of responsibility. Of course, you should make sure he gets paid in stars, check marks, money, or rewards for his efforts.

• **Include educational and recreational activities.**   Some parents assign a fifteen-to-thirty-minute school-related task to their child three or four times per week and offer her a reward for doing it. If you're interested in including this kind of task as part of your child's summer Game, you can have your child read, do math problems, and/or learn about current events, science, or history. Try to make the activity fun, encourage your child to pay attention, and make certain to reward her efforts. You can also include participating in recreational and sports activities.

• **Keep working on areas that need improvement.**   If you were already focusing on a certain kind of behavior during the spring, it's usually a good idea to continue working on it during the summer. If your child needs to work on an academic problem in reading or math or if he needs help with his speech or physical coordination, summer is a good time to include activities that will help him improve in these places. If your child wants to improve at a sport, summer is also a good time for that.

• **Focus on a new behavior or challenge.**   And, if you feel like it's the right time, you may also want to introduce something new that your child needs to work on. The summer can be a good time to begin working on things that are going to take a while for your child to adjust to. For instance, if it's time for your child to get braces, the summer is a good time to start. If he needs to wear glasses or get used to contacts, consider doing that during the summer.

• **Double-check your child's Reward Chart.**   Since your child is likely to have more free time during the summer, you may want to encourage her to use this time in a variety of ways. One way to do this is to limit the length of time she can spend at any one activity. For example, you might want to specify how much time she can watch television and play video games. You may also need to make sure certain chores are done and/or certain school-related tasks have been completed before your child can cash in her check marks and buy her rewards. Summer can also be a good time for your child to earn more money, save it up, and get something she really wants.

As a special reward during the summer you may want to plan some fun activities with your child. These might be outings you don't have a chance to take during the school year, such as going to a sports game or an amusement park. You can also consider letting your child go to day or overnight camp as a big reward.

• **Keep your discipline plan the same.**   Continue to use warnings, ignoring, time-out, the quiet chair, and taking away things or privileges the same way that you have throughout the rest of the year. Don't lighten up and let your children fall back into bad habits like arguing and fighting all the time.

• **Make up your child's summer Game.**   Once you and your child have talked about his good behavior and rewards and whether you want to add anything for the summer, it's time to fill out a revised Good Behavior Chart and Reward Chart for your child. Have these ready for your summer checkup meeting.

Getting Started

To make certain that everyone understands how the summer Game will work, here are some guidelines to follow:

• **Have an official summer checkup meeting.**   Hold your meeting on the Sunday either right before or right after school is finished.

• **Talk about what happened during the spring.**   Review how the winter and spring went and focus on the positive developments. Encourage your family to share experiences they enjoyed over the past several months.

• **Go over the revised Game and how it will work.**   Quickly review each behavior and reward, stopping to highlight any changes that have been made. Be sure to review anything special you want your child to work on. When reviewing her rewards, make sure your child understands any limitations on free time as well as any opportunities to earn extra money.

• **Put your child's chart up and get started.**   Just as you have every other week, put up his chart and begin the Game for the next week.

• **Do something fun at the end of the meeting.**   Celebrate the end of the school year and the beginning of summer. Have a treat, a special dinner, or go to a movie. You deserve it, your family made it through another school year!

• **Monitor your Game.**   As you have before, during the first several weeks watch carefully to make sure your summer Game is working. Keep an eye on your children and make sure they're not sleeping too late, lying around all day watching television, and never getting any physical activity. And, whatever you do, don't let them turn into misbehaving couch potatoes.

• **Enjoy the free time you have with your child.**   One of the best parts about summer can be hanging out and enjoying doing "nothing" with your child. Take advantage of your free time and spend it with your child. Enjoy your family's release from the stresses and pressures of school. Have fun together.

Let's see how my clients Bud and Nancy Galleon made up their daughter Erica's summer Game:

Bud and Nancy felt that their ten-year-old daughter Erica needed some time off from the pressures of school, so when they made up her summer Game they relaxed their standards wherever they could. When they talked to Erica about their plans for her summer Game, she loved the idea of getting to stay up later and being able to sleep in longer. But she wanted to make sure that she continued to earn rewards and save up her money. Bud reassured her that there would be plenty of opportunities to earn check marks. She could continue helping around the house, feeding the pets, and spending some time every day reading a book or the newspaper. Erica and her dad also decided that as a special reward, Erica could go to the day camp of her choice for a week or two.

As a reminder, your next big-picture checkup is scheduled for the fall when school is starting, so when that time arrives again, please refer to the beginning of this chapter for guidelines to follow as you do your fall checkup.

WRAPPING IT UP AND SAYING GOOD-BYE

Even though you've reached the end of this book, as you're aware, your journey is far from over. As you face the ongoing challenges of raising your child day by day for the coming years, I strongly recommend that you keep the Behavior Game close by and continue playing it for as long as it's helpful.

Let's take a last look at the Bradley family as they continue playing the Game:

Whenever Joan or Gary Bradley asked Cindy and Bobby if they wanted to stop playing the Game, their children's "no" was immediate and definite. Cindy and Bobby wanted to keep playing the Game and earning rewards. In fact, Cindy often told her parents that she intended to play the Game for the rest of her life or at least until she went off to college. While Joan and Gary were pretty sure that Cindy wouldn't want a Good Behavior Chart posted on the refrigerator when she was a teenager, they didn't contradict her. The important thing was that rewards continued to motivate Cindy to behave better. Cindy was doing things that seemed impossible for her even several months earlier. She was getting along with her brother Bobby most of the time. She was offering to help out. She was pleasant at meals. Gone were the incessant back talk and surly attitude. Cindy was much nicer to be around, usually pleasant and civil even to her mom. Bobby continued to make good changes as well. In particular, he was much more responsible about getting up in the morning and doing his schoolwork. As Joan and Gary thought about it, they realized they had no reason to stop playing. For as long as Cindy and Bobby wanted, they'd continue with the Game.

There is no recommended minimum or maximum amount of time to use the Game. Different families need the Game for different times. Just because your neighbor or best friend has stopped using the Game, don't let that influence your decision. Use the Game until you feel you don't need it anymore, whether it's six months or six years.

With my children I used a Behavior Game chart for over six years, probably more like seven or eight years. I started with a very simple chart when my first son was two and had to wear glasses, which needless to say he didn't want to do. Fortunately, earning stickers and treats for putting on his glasses and keeping them on worked. Over the years I continued using a chart to help my children succeed at all the normal daily behavior I wanted to see in them from the time they got up until the time they went to bed. I didn't stop using the chart until my children actually suggested it. When they no longer wanted a chart and didn't seem to need one any longer, we stopped using a formal chart and switched to a performance-based allowance, which proved to be enough to help them get things done. With your child, use your judgment and continue your child's chart for as long as you feel it's helping.

And remember, if it turns out you stopped the Game too soon, you can always start it up again. You might stop using the Game for a while and everything will go fine, and then gradually behavior gets worse and worse. If this happens, you can always reintroduce the Game and use it again.

As your child gets older, she may want to stop using the Game. If your child asks to stop, you can discontinue the Game and see what happens. If she's able to behave as you want her to without needing a chart and check marks, that's great. She probably doesn't need an official chart anymore. Let's see what happened to my former clients Doreen and Lonnie Fitzgerald when they stopped playing the Game with their daughter Georgia.

After playing the Game for three years, Georgia Fitzgerald, age eleven, announced that she was ready to stop using her chart. She told her parents that she wanted to trade in her chart for an old-fashioned weekly allowance. Since Georgia was good about getting up and getting ready in the morning and was very organized about her schoolwork and chores, the time seemed right. After agreeing on what she needed to do to earn her allowance, Georgia, Doreen, and Lonnie decided to give this new plan a try. As it turned out, Georgia was ready. She did very well and needed only an occasional reminder to finish her schoolwork.

Although your child is likely to be gung ho now, as he approaches his teen years, he's likely to lose enthusiasm for a formal chart and may instead opt for an allowance to compensate him for his efforts and hard work. But even when it's time to take your child's chart down from the refrigerator, don't forsake the basics of the Game. No matter how old your child is, he'll never outgrow his need for your attention, support, encouragement, and praise, so keep rewarding. And don't forget the importance of using structure and limits when your child misbehaves. Children and teens alike benefit when you enforce consequences for their problem behavior.

Over the years the families I've worked with have shown me again and again how the Behavior Game with its special combination of rewards and limits can help parents develop a solid foundation upon which to build a lasting and wonderful relationship with their children. In fact, I am reminded of my ever-changing relationship with my older son, one of the true guinea pigs of the Behavior Game. Off at college for his freshman year, as I write this, we're all trying to adjust to his first year away from home, a difficult and awesome task at best. Although we've had our ups and downs as all families do, we can still talk and share the good and bad. Recently on an especially bad day for him, he called and confided in me that he hadn't realized how important his family was until he went away to college. After I finally finished crying, it struck me how infrequently children tell their parents how much they appreciate what their parents have done. My son's heartfelt sentiments inspired this closing thought.

Hang in there and keep up the good work, your efforts will pay off. And if your children haven't already told you, let me say this for them, "Thanks for everything, Mom and Dad. Now and forever."

APPENDIX A
FORMS TO COPY

Feel free to copy these forms for your use.

Good Behavior Checklist
Reward Checklist
Parent Reward Checklist
Good Behavior Chart
Reward Chart
Parent Daily Checklist
Discipline Plan

Good Behavior Checklist

For _____

Instructions: Indicate whether your child displays each kind of behavior "often," "sometimes," "rarely," or "never." If you're not sure how frequently a particular kind of behavior occurs, spend a few more days watching your child.

MORNING BEHAVIOR	OFTEN	SOMETIMES	RARELY	NEVER
Getting up on time				
Getting dressed without a hassle				
Taking care of self				
Eating breakfast nicely				
Being ready for school				
Other				

DAILY BEHAVIOR	OFTEN	SOMETIMES	RARELY	NEVER
Getting along with brothers or sisters				
Getting along with friends				
Getting along with Mom or Dad				
Doing what is asked				
Doing chores				
Doing schoolwork				
Eating dinner nicely				
Other				

BEDTIME BEHAVIOR	OFTEN	SOMETIMES	RARELY	NEVER
Getting ready for bed on time				
Going to bed on time				
Staying in bed				
Other				

Reward Checklist

For _____

Instructions: Check each reward that you want to include in your child's Behavior Game.

DAILY REWARDS

15 minutes of free time
- ☐ Be with Mom or Dad
- ☐ Read a story
- ☐ Play a game
- ☐ Go for a walk
- ☐ Play with toys
- ☐ Watch television
- ☐ Listen to music
- ☐ Talk on telephone

Other fun things
- ☐ _____
- ☐ _____
- ☐ _____

Food treat
- ☐ _____
- ☐ _____

Being with friends
- ☐ Have a friend over
- ☐ Visit a friend
- ☐ Other _____

Bedtime rewards
- ☐ Extra bedtime story
- ☐ Stay up 30 minutes later
- ☐ Other _____

Earning money
- ☐ For good behaviors

Other rewards
- ☐ _____
- ☐ _____

WEEKLY REWARDS

Weekend activities
- ☐ With Mom or Dad
- ☐ With friends
- ☐ See a movie
- ☐ Go out to lunch
- ☐ Have a friend overnight
- ☐ Go to a friend's house

Other fun things
- ☐ _____
- ☐ _____
- ☐ _____

Getting something new
- ☐ An affordable toy/game/book
- ☐ Rent a game or video
- ☐ Sports item
- ☐ Clothes, stuff to wear

Other new stuff to get
- ☐ _____
- ☐ _____
- ☐ _____

MONTHLY REWARDS

Saving up for
- ☐ _____
- ☐ _____

Other rewards
- ☐ _____
- ☐ _____

Parent Reward Checklist

For _____

Instructions: The following list contains rewards that my clients have enjoyed. Check off those things and activities you'd like to include as your own rewards. Add any others as well.

DAILY REWARDS

☐ Take a walk, get some exercise

☐ Watch television, write a letter, talk to a friend, listen to music

☐ Read a book, look at the newspaper, flip through a magazine

☐ Fool around with your computer, learn about something new

☐ Cook, sew, or garden

☐ Work on the car or a home-improvement project

☐ Just do nothing for a few moments

☐ Other

WEEKLY REWARDS

☐ Try to get away for a few hours, go somewhere, and do something

☐ Go out for dinner, see a movie, go shopping

☐ Play a sport, go on a long walk

☐ Just do something fun or do nothing at all

☐ Other _____

Good Behavior Chart

For _____ / From _____ To ____

GOOD BEHAVIOR	SUN.	MON.	TUES.	WED.	THURS.	FRI.	SAT.
Getting up on time (___)							
Getting dressed							
Taking care of self							
Eating breakfast nicely							
Being ready for school (___)							
Other							
Getting along with • Brother/sister (___min.)							
• Friends (___min.)							
• Parents (___min.)							
Doing what is asked							
Doing chores							
•							
•							
Doing schoolwork (__min.)							
•							
•							
Eating dinner nicely							
Other							
Getting ready for bed (___)							
Going to bed (___)							
Staying in bed							
Other							
Daily Total							

	Weekly Total	

Reward Chart

For _____ / From _____ To _____

DAILY REWARDS			WEEKLY REWARDS		
15 minutes free time	**Cost**	**x/Day**	**Weekend activities**	**Cost**	**x/Wk**
Be with Mom/Dad	____	____	With Mom/Dad	____	____
Read a story	____	____	With friends	____	____
Play a game	____	____	See a movie	____	____
Go for a walk	____	____	Rent movie/game	____	____
Play with toys	____	____	Go to lunch	____	____
Watch television	____	____	Have friend overnight	____	____
Listen to music	____	____	Visit friend	____	____
Talk on phone	____	____	Other _____	____	____
Other_____	____	____	_____	____	____
_____	____	____	_____	____	____
			_____	____	____
Food treat	____	____			
_____	____	____	**Getting something new and affordable**		
			Game, toy, book	____	____
Being with friends			Sports item	____	____
Have friend over	____	____	Clothes	____	____
Visit a friend	____	____	Other _____	____	____
Other _____	____	____	_____	____	____
Bedtime rewards			_____	____	____
Extra story	____	____	_____	____	____
Stay up 30 min. extra	____	____			
Other _____	____	____			

Being with friends
Have friend over
Visit a friend
Other _____

Bedtime rewards
Extra story
Stay up 30 min. extra
Other _____

Other rewards ____ ____
_____ ____ ____

Weekly Cash-in Times
During weekend as needed

Getting money
Each star/check mark = ____
Maximum earned each day = ____

Daily Cash-in Times	
After school	Before bed
Before dinner	As needed

MONTHLY REWARDS		
Saving up for	**Cost**	**x/Mon**
_____	____	____
_____	____	____
_____	____	____
_____	____	____
_____	____	____

Parent Daily Checklist

EVERY DAY, THROUGHOUT THE DAY . . .

Adopt a calm, positive attitude.

Talk with your child about the Game.

Give frequent advance notices, reminders, and help.

Praise your child for good behavior.

Put stars or check marks on your child's chart.

Provide enough cash-in times.

Give yourself credit for your efforts.

When possible, enjoy a reward from your list.

IN THE MORNING . . .

Wake up early so your family has time to get ready.

Let your children know what they need to do.

Remind them they can spend their stars after school.

IN THE AFTERNOON . . .

If you're home with your children:

Get in the right frame of mind.

After school, allow time for sharing the day's experiences.

Offer an after-school cash-in time.

Go over what everyone has to do and get each one started.

When possible, take short breaks and offer cash-in times.

If you work and get home around dinnertime:

When you get home, allow time for sharing the day's experiences.

Offer a before-dinner cash-in time (if possible).

If there's time, have your children begin schoolwork.

AT DINNERTIME . . .

Prepare your family for a peaceful dinner.

Let everyone know when each is doing well.

IN THE EVENING . . .

Map out everyone's schedule and get each one started.

Monitor progress and offer cash-in times when needed.

AT BEDTIME . . .

Remind your child when it's time to get ready for bed and what needs to be done.

After your child is ready for bed, take some additional time to discuss the day's experiences.

Offer a final cash-in time when your child can buy a before-bed reward.

Give an advance notice before bedtime.

Make sure your child goes to bed on time.

ONCE YOUR CHILD IS IN BED . . .

Pat yourself on the back.

Review your day and look ahead to tomorrow.

Congratulate yourself—you made it through another day!

ON THE WEEKEND . . .

Play a relaxed version of the Behavior Game.

Be sure your child has a chance to enjoy his or her weekly rewards.

Enjoy your own weekly reward.

Discipline Plan

For _____

Instructions: Put a check beside each problem your child continues to have, and then fill in which discipline techniques you plan to use. Be sure to consider warnings, ignoring, time-out, the quiet chair, and taking away a privilege or possession for a short time.

☐	Not getting up on time
☐	Not getting dressed without a hassle
☐	Not taking care of self
☐	Not eating breakfast nicely
☐	Not being ready for school on time
☐	Not getting along with brothers/sisters
☐	Not getting along with friends
☐	Not getting along with parents
☐	Not doing what is asked
☐	Not doing chores
☐	Not doing schoolwork
☐	Not eating dinner nicely
☐	Not getting ready for bed
☐	Not going to bed
☐	Not staying in bed
☐	Other

APPENDIX B
FURTHER READING

The books listed below contain additional practical suggestions concerning topics covered in this book.

More about Discipline Techniques

The following books contain additional ideas for using discipline techniques with specific problem behavior:

Garber, Stephen, Garber, Marianne, and Spizman, Robyn. *Good Behavior: Over 1200 Sensible Solutions to Your Child's Problems from Birth to Age Twelve.* New York: St. Martin's Press, 1991.

Nelsen, Jane, Lott, Lynn, and Glenn, H. Stephen. *Positive Discipline, A to Z, 1001 Solutions to Everyday Parenting Problems.* Rocklin, Calif.: Prima Press, 1993.

Windell, James. *Discipline: A Sourcebook of 50 Failsafe Techniques for Parents.* New York: Collier, 1991.

More about Homework

The following books contain practical tips on helping your child get his homework done without a fight.

Clark, F., and Clark, C. *Hasslefree Homework: A Six-Week Plan for Parents and Children to Take the Pain out of Homework.* New York: Doubleday & Co., 1989.

Morison, K., and Brady, S. *Homework: Bridging the Gap.* Redmond, Wash.: Goodfellow Press, 1994.

Rosemond, John. *Ending the Homework Hassle.* New York: Andrews and McMeel, 1992.

More about Siblings

These books offer ideas about how to help brothers and sisters get along.

Ames, Louise B., and Haber, C. C. *He Hit Me First.* New York: Warner Books, 1982.

Faber, Adele, and Mazlish, Elaine. *Siblings Without Rivalry.* New York: Avon, 1987.

More about School Problems

These books are excellent resources for parents who are searching for ways to help their child with school.

Martin, Michael, and Waltman-Greenwood, Cynthia, ed. *Solve Your Child's School-Related Problems.* New York: HarperCollins, 1995.

Novick, B. Z., and Arnold, M. *Why Is My Child Having Trouble in School? A Parent's Guide to Learning Disabilities.* New York: Jeremy P. Tarcher/Putnam Books, 1991.

More about Divorced Parents, Co-Parents, and Stepparents

These books offer practical tips on the very tricky and complicated subject of parenting after divorce.

Berman, Claire. *Making It as a Stepparent.* New York: Doubleday, 1986.

Blau, Melinda. *Ten Keys to Successful Co-Parenting.* New York: Perigee Books, 1993.

Gardner, Richard A. *Parent's Book about Divorce.* New York: Bantam Books, 1991.

Hickey, E., and Dalton, E. *Helping Children and Adults Recover from Divorce.* Carson City, Nev.: Gold Leaf Press, 1994.

More about Working Parents

These books provide practical suggestions for the working parent who's trying to do it all.

Nigro, Debbie. *The Working Mom on the Run Manual.* New York: Master Media, 1995.

Price, Susan C., and Price, Tom. *The Working Parent's Help Book*. Princeton, N.J.: Petersens Books, 1994.

More about Communication, Problem Solving, and Thinking

These books give you further tips on communicating with your child and helping him solve problems and conflicts.

Crary, Elizabeth. *A Practical Guide to Teaching Problem Solving*. Seattle: Parenting Press, 1984.

Eastman, Meg. *Taming the Dragon in Your Child: Solutions for Breaking the Cycle of Family Anger*. New York: John Wiley & Sons, Inc., 1994.

Faber, Adele, and Mazlish, Elaine. *How to Talk So Kids Will Listen and Listen So Kids Will Talk*. New York: Avon Books, 1980.

Shure, Myrna B. *Raising a Thinking Child: Help Your Young Child to Resolve Everyday Conflicts*. New York: Henry Holt & Co., 1994.

More about Self-esteem

These books offer down-to-earth suggestions about how to ensure that your child develops positive self-esteem as she grows up.

Rosenberg, Ellen. *Growing Up Feeling Good*. New York: Puffin, 1987.

Stitt, Julie. *The Parenting Tightrope: A Flexible Approach to Building Self-Esteem*. Troy, Mich.: Momentum Books, 1994.

More about Dealing with Normal Problems

These books look at normal problems and how you can help your child solve them.

Turecki, Stanley. *Normal Children Have Problems, Too: How Parents Can Understand and Help*. New York: Bantum Books, 1994.

Youngs, Bettie. *Stress and Your Child: Helping Kids Cope with the Strains and Pressures of Life*. New York: Fawcett Columbine, 1985.

APPENDIX C
GETTING PROFESSIONAL HELP

Finding the right professional to help your child is not always easy. In my clinical work I've found that no matter how elaborate and thorough a referral system I develop, I need to revise and add to it constantly, partly because my clients have ever-changing needs and partly because the resources that exist change so quickly. Since each client's search is unique, I feel most comfortable giving you general, rather than specific, guidelines to help you get started. If possible don't hurry your search. Of course, if you're faced with a situation in which there's danger for your child or others and emergency service is needed, such as in the case of suicidal behavior, take immediate action, call your doctor or your local hospital, and get help now. But otherwise, spend time weighing your options and deciding the best way to proceed.

As you learned in chapter 8, the best place to begin your search for help is usually with professionals who currently care for your child. Ask your child's pediatrician or your family doctor for advice and referrals. If she's stumped, try contacting your child's teacher or school counselor. Many parents find it helpful to talk with friends, especially those who have consulted a therapist. If you're involved in a community activity, church, temple, or synagogue, check with the staff to find out if they have a recommendation about who can help you.

And for some of my clients, even the phone book has proven helpful. Currently many phone books contain a section on local health and mental health services as well as hotlines to call in emergencies. These up-to-date listings of community services can give you places to call and get started in your search. If you have a local mental health association, contact it for referrals as well. If none of these avenues works, you can contact national or state associations for their ideas and recommendations. These organizations keep a list of members by location and specialty.

Here is a list of associations you may find helpful:

American Academy of Pediatrics
141 Northwest Point Boulevard
Elk Grove Village, IL 60007
708-228-5005

American Psychological Association
750 First Street, N.E.
Washington, DC 20002
800-374-2721

National Association of Social Workers
750 First Street, N.E., Suite 700
Washington, DC 20002
800-638-8799

American Psychiatric Association
1400 K Street, N.W.
Washington, DC 20005
202-682-6000

Association for Children with Learning Disabilities
4156 Library Road
Pittsburgh, PA 15234
412-341-1515

As you search, try to be patient, creative, persistent, and optimistic. For all you know help may be just around the corner. Good luck in your search. I've got my fingers crossed and know you'll keep looking because after all your kids are worth it.

APPENDIX D
THEORETICAL FOUNDATIONS OF THE BEHAVIOR GAME

The following books and articles on social learning theory and behavior therapy influenced the original Behavior Game as well as helped it evolve:

Bandura, Albert. *Principles of Behavior Modification*. New York: Holt, Rinehart and Winston, 1969.

———. *Social Learning Theory*. Englewood Cliffs, N.J.: Prentice Hall, 1977.

———. *Social Foundations of Thought and Action: A Social Cognitive Theory*. Englewood Cliffs, N.J.: Prentice Hall, 1986.

Krumboltz, John D., and Krumboltz, Helen B. *Changing Children's Behavior*. Englewood Cliffs, N.J.: Prentice Hall, 1972.

Meichenbaum, Donald. *Cognitive-Behavior Modification*. New York: Plenum Publishing, 1977.

Mischel, Walter. *Personality and Assessment*. New York: John Wiley & Sons, 1968.

———. *Introduction to Personality*. New York: Holt, Rinehart and Winston, 1971.

———. "Toward a Cognitive Social Learning Reconceptualization of Personality," *Psychological Review* 80 (1973):252–83.

O'Leary, K. Daniel, and Wilson, G. Terence. *Behavior Therapy: Outcome and Application, 2nd ed.* Englewood Cliffs, N.J.: Prentice Hall, 1987.

Rosenthal, Ted L. "Social Learning Theory and Behavior Therapy." In *Contemporary Behavior Therapy: Conceptual and Empirical Foundations*, edited by G. Terence Wilson and Cyril M. Franks. New York: Guilford Press, 1982.

Ullmann, Leonard P., and Krasner, Leonard, ed. *Case Studies in Behavior Modification*. New York: Holt, Rinehart and Winston, 1965.

INDEX

203

bedtime *(continued)*
  and staying in bed, 18, 49, 71
  story reading, 32
begging, ignoring, 93, 104
behavior. *See* good behavior;
      irritating behaviors; problem
      behavior; *specific types of
      behavior*
Behavior Game
  age range for, 6, 163
  child's balking at, 79
  deciding when to stop, 181–82
  and Discipline Plan, 107, 110–
      11
  explaining to child, 76
  in fall, 170–74
  first day of, 78
  first week of, 79–81
  goal of, 5, 11–12
  including other adults, 127–34
  incorporating into daily life, 64–
      74
  initiating, 75–81
  making up child's Behavior
      Game, 40–63
  for older children, 163–66, 182
  outside the house, 122–26
  participants, 6–7
  and problem behaviors, 12, 89–
      115
  refinements in, 116–22
  reviewing and revising weekly,
      84–86
  reviewing positive changes,
      151–56
  reviewing seasonally, 169
  reward system, 22–39, 53–63
  in summer, 179–80

  on weekends, 83
  in winter, 174–77
  See also Good Behavior Chart;
      Reward Chart
bossiness, child's, 161
breakfast, 17, 45, 103
breaks, after-school, 68
bribes, 23
brothers. *See* siblings
bullying, 162

calming down. *See* cooling off
cash-in times
  for daily rewards, 56–57
  during the day, 56–57, 68–70
  explaining, 76
  for monthly rewards, 59
  opportunities for, 65
  for preschool children, 63
  at start of Behavior Game, 78
  on weekends, 72
  for weekly rewards, 58–59, 72
celebrating Behavior Game
      progress, 167–78
charts. *See* Good Behavior Chart;
      Reward Chart
cheating, 162
checklists. *See* Good Behavior
      Checklist; Parent Daily
      Checklist; Parent Reward
      Checklist; Reward Checklist
check marks. *See* stars and check
      marks
chores
  adding to number of, 120
  doing without reminders, 17
  increasing during summer, 177–78
  not doing, 12, 105